Praise for
The Way of Life

"Short, shrewd, and encouraging reflections on our need to seek holiness, and on how to do it."

—Fr. Thomas Crean, O.P.

"Better to light a candle than to curse the darkness (or so it is said), but Phillip Campbell does both in addressing a wide range of issues of concern to Catholics who take seriously God's universal call to holiness. These essays are clearsighted, discerning, challenging, and steeped in the Catholic spiritual tradition—an act of faith in the transformative power of grace in the individual soul and the abiding presence of the Holy Spirit in the Church."

—Fr. Thomas Kocik

"One of the compelling themes running throughout this collection of essays is the need for ordinary Catholics to practice greater mortifications. This is not so much the conclusion of learned argumentation as it is the practical wisdom gained through reflection on the experience of striving and struggling for real growth in virtue, and it is all the more eloquent for that. If you find yourself easily drawn into fruitless fretting about the state of affairs in the Church or in the world, this book will help you to refocus your attention on the one thing necessary, which is to deny yourself, take up your cross daily, and follow after Jesus Christ on the way of life."

—Dr. John Joy

"I have often benefited from reading Campbell's wise and gritty reflections, the fruits of a life marked with hardship, a heart steeped in Catholic tradition, and a mind always looking for light. These essays are especially helpful for Catholics who feel seasick in the storm-tossed boat of today's Church, wondering when the Captain of the bark will rise up to calm the waves. Campbell helps us to see that He is still and always in control and we can enter into His rest."

—Dr. Peter Kwasniewski

The Way of Life

The
Way of Life

Spiritual Essays from Unam Sanctam Catholicam

Phillip Campbell
with Noah Moerbeek, CPMO

AROUCA
PRESS

These essays were first published at the Unam Sanctam
Catholicam blog between 2010–2022. Chapters 21, 37, and 39
are unpublished essays and are included here for the first time.
Chapters 9, 17, and 24 were written by Noah Moerbeek. A list
of the dates of composition are included in the appendix.

ISBN: 978-1-990685-57-6 (pbk)
ISBN: 978-1-990685-58-3 (hc)

Arouca Press
PO Box 55003
Bridgeport PO
Waterloo, ON N2J 3G0
Canada
www.aroucapress.com
Send inquiries to info@aroucapress.com

Book and cover design by
Emma Nagle

Cover image licensed free for use through Pixabay

This book is dedicated to my friend and mentor, Dr. Philip Blosser for his years of friendship and support of my writing.

I would also like to thank dom Noah Moerbeek for his contributions, as well as all the fine people who reviewed it and provided valuable feedback. Special thanks to Alexandros Barbas for giving me the opportunity to bring this to print, and much love and gratitude to all the readers of Unam Sanctam Catholicam over the years who have kept the site afloat.

Table of Contents

Introduction

❧

"There are two ways, one of life and one of death; but a great difference between the two ways." Thus begins the *Didache*, perhaps the earliest Christian text outside the New Testament. Christianity is a vast concept encompassing various realities: it is a system of beliefs, a liturgical tradition, a moral code, and a cultural heritage, to name a few. But what always strikes me about the *Didache* is its description of Christianity as a "way"—specifically, a way of life.

We may ask: what is meant by this phrase, way of life? Is it a way of life in the sense of a manner of living, or is it rather a way that leads to life? Is "the way" something we do now, or is it a path that leads us somewhere else? The answer is both.

The *Didache* is not the only Christian text to conceive of the faith as a "way." The phrase originates with Jesus Christ Himself, who said, "For the gate is narrow and the way is hard, that leads to life, and those who find it are few" (Matt. 7:14). Elsewhere, He identifies Himself as the way: "Jesus saith unto him, I am the way, and the truth, and the life" (John 14:6).

We know that in Antioch the believers were first called Christians (cf. Acts 11:26), but before this name became universal, "the Way" was used as another name for the faith. The Book of Acts is full of references to Christianity as "the Way," both in terms of its beliefs and structure. While still a Pharisee, Saul went to Damascus "so that if he found any belonging to the Way...he might bring them bound to Jerusalem" (9:2). The evangelist Apollos was said to be "instructed in the way of the Lord;" when Priscilla and Aquila heard him speaking in Corinth, "they took him and expounded to him the way of God more accurately" (18:26). In Philippi, the demon possessed slave girl cried out against St. Paul and Silas, "These men are servants of the Most High God, who proclaim to you the way of salvation" (16:17). St. Luke says incredulous Jews in Corinth "refused to believe and publicly maligned the Way" (19:9); in the same chapter, Luke recalls that in Ephesus "about that time there arose no little stir concerning the Way" (19:23). And St. Paul told the procurator Felix at his hearing, "This I admit to you, that according to the Way, which they call a sect, I worship the God of our fathers, believing everything laid down by the law or written in the prophets" (24:14). Compare this to the terms Christian or Christians, which are only used three times in the entire New Testament. It appears that "the Way" was the favored manner of referring to the faith, at least in primitive times.

What does it mean to consider our faith as a "way?" Several things are implied: it is a road upon which we travel, but it is also the journey itself. It is a manner of living, but also a name descriptive of those who follow the said manner of living. If the Gospel is our standard, it implies certain thoughts, attitudes, and ethical norms. To put it simply, the Way is the faith considered as the sum of its parts—Catholicism in its glorious totality, both in its execution and its perfection.

In recent years, amidst the chaos in the Church and the fractious liturgy wars, I have spent more time meditating on Christianity as "the Way," to great benefit. There is a deep thirst for a more wholistic experience of the faith in the Church today. This is ultimately what the traditionalist movement is all about: laboring for a Catholicism that goes beyond something we do on Sunday, for something that is transformative, penetrating to the bone and marrow of society—culture, economics, family life, government, the arts, and every aspect of human activity. Centered on the liturgy, which encapsulates everything the Church lives and believes, we desire a Catholicism that is truly universal in the most profound sense. This also relates to the essential critique of contemporary Catholicism: it doesn't go deep enough. Despite all the gimmicks—all the outreach committees, liturgical coordinators, parish revitalization programs, and all the *talking*—despite it all, it fails to answer our Lord's call to "put out into the deep" (cf. Luke 5:4). We search for an inheritance and are given pottage; we cry for bread and are handed a stone; we seek a Way and are offered a "lifehack."

This gets to the heart of the Church's modern crisis. Traditional Catholics are not mere aesthetes who fawn over the ancient liturgy for its smells and bells; we desire it because of its superior ability to nurture our spiritual life— it is a surer way to God, our final end and the source of all good. If the traditional liturgy did not facilitate a deeper union with God, of what advantage would it be? Thus we prefer the integrity of tradition to the fractured mess of modernity.

But we, too, are not immune from the same tendencies we decry. We, too, can treat the faith like a program, a series of ten easy steps to be implemented while neglecting weightier matters (cf. Matt. 23:23). We can fail to see the forest for the trees, clutching to fragments of truth that prevent us from seeing the whole. We can be so indignant at the injustice in the world that we stress justice till we lose sight of mercy. We can insist on God's transcendent otherness so vehemently that we lose sense of His closeness. We can dwell on the punishment of sinners to the degree that we neglect to recall God's desire to save. We can emphasize suffering to the point that we forget that God made us for happiness. And we can become so overwhelmed with themes of penitence and chastisement that we forget how to "rejoice in the Lord always" (Phil. 4:4).

Many Catholics these days are discouraged. This is understandable; from a human perspective, there is little room for optimism. Not only the world but the Church itself seems bent on self-destruction. Dark clouds are gathering; everyone has a sense of impending doom. The inability to process these things has led to real loss of faith among many. How can we find our way back when we have come so far, when so many bad things have happened?

"With God, all things are possible," our Lord tells us (Matt. 19:26). One of the most consoling episodes in the Scriptures is Ezekiel's vision in the valley of dry bones in Ezekiel 37. The Lord takes Ezekiel to a barren valley littered with the bones of the slain. Strewn about the rocky landscape of this dusty valley, we can imagine the thousands of bleached skulls with their empty, hollow sockets staring blankly at the prophet. The wind sweeps over the desolate waste, rattling the pale bones as it passes. It is a place of dryness—of desiccation and death.

But such is not the perspective of God. Where Ezekiel sees death, the Lord sees possibility. He asks the prophet, "Son of man, can these bones live?" (Ezek. 37:3) Ezekiel replies, "Lord, you know." The Lord looks out at this desolation and says, "Behold, I will cause breath to enter you, and you shall live. And I will lay sinews upon you, and will cause flesh to come upon you, and cover you with skin, and put breath in you, and you shall live; and you shall know that I am the LORD." (Ezek. 37:5–6). And so it was: the bones began to rattle, then come together, bound by sinews and muscle that sprang forth, and were wrapped about in human flesh which, when blown upon by the four winds, became a host of living men, vivified by the Spirit of the living God.

Is the situation any different today? When we survey the chaos of the world, we are like Ezekiel, brought up to the high place overlooking the valley of dry bones. Surveying the disasters of our own day, God says to each of us, "Son of man, can these bones live?" How do we answer? Do we see only failure, the absence of vitality? Or do we see raw potential? Do we perceive an end, or a beginning? Are the dry bones a terminus point, or a foundation stone? Look out at the bones and ask yourself, "Can these bones live? Yes, or no?" And you will see how everything changes depending on your answer.

Our Lord tells us we need eyes to see (Matt. 13:15). In the Beatitudes, He says, "The eye is the lamp of the body; so then if your eye is clear, your whole body will be full of light" (Matt. 6:22). The light Jesus requires of us is the gift of understanding, by which we see beyond mere externals, and St. Thomas Aquinas beautifully explains understanding as a supernatural light that takes us beyond mere reason:

> The stronger the light of the understanding, the further can it penetrate into the heart of things. Now the natural light of our understanding is of finite power; wherefore it can reach to a certain fixed point. Consequently man needs a supernatural light in order to penetrate further still so as to know what it cannot know by its natural light: and this supernatural light which is bestowed on man is called the gift of understanding. (*ST*, II-II, q. 8, a. 1)

Illumined by this light, what do we see in the valley of dry bones? We see possibility. We see that the Way is as sure as it ever was. "Behold, the Lord's hand is not shortened, that it cannot save, or his ear dull, that it cannot hear" (Isa. 59:1).

To be sure, the distractions are greater today: Christianity competes not merely against rival ideologies, but against an entire system of life constructed upon ephemerality, ease, and entertainment. These distractions are so ubiquitous we may be tempted to despair, but we must view them through the light of faith. In God's order, challenges exist to be wrestled with and overcome; hurdles exist that we might learn to leap. We may deplore that we have these particular hurdles to jump; we may wish we could have been born in some better age. But God could have placed you anywhere in any time and He chose to place you *here* and *now*. That should be a tremendous consolation. He wants you to live the faith in *this* time, in *this* age. The Way, like Christ, is incarnational—it must be "enfleshed" in every generation, lived heroically in the midst of whatever Cross that history has meted out to us.

How can we walk the way of life in a world where the society is antithetical to our values and the Church gives little support? This is a very large question, one which I have been grappling with for the last two decades. The essays in this book summarize my reflections on various facets of this subject over the years. Most of these essays were originally published between 2010 and 2023 on my blog and website Unam Sanctam Catholicam (although a few are being published for the first time here). The majority are my own, but a handful were written by dom Noah Moerbeek, CPMO, a dear friend and brother in the Lord whose commitment to the spiritual life has always been a source of inspiration to me.

The essays will speak for themselves so I will not waste time with a thematic introduction, though I will offer a word about their arrangement: My original intent was to simply present the essays in chronological order, but in the end I chose to mix them up so the subject matter would be more diverse and the evolution of my writing style over thirteen years would not be so obvious.

Finally, a disclaimer: I am no spiritual master by any means; I am a layman trying to muddle my way through the vicissitudes of life with the light Christ has given me. I chose to allow Arouca Press to publish these essays because many readers over the years have told me they have been helped by them. It is my hope that these essays may, in some way, also help you along the way of life.

Phillip Campbell
April 2, 2023
Palm Sunday

1

Balancing Truth and Humility

❧

" The truth shall set you free," our Lord promises in the Gospel (John 8:32). To stand in the truth gives one's life stability, direction, and purpose. It gives balance to our spiritual lives and prevents us from "from being tossed to and fro by every wind of doctrine" (Eph. 4:14). The desire for truth is inherent in human nature; as Aristotle observed, "All men by nature desire to know." This is a consequent of our rational nature imparted to us by God.

The subjective possession of truth, however, can work strangely in us. Universal human experience reveals that often there are no more intransigent people than those convinced that they are right. Whether they actually are right matters little—the subjective *belief* that one is right is enough. Arguing with a person who is utterly certain of their rectitude can be endlessly frustrating. Such experiences demonstrate that, though truth can set us free, it can also make one arrogant. The universality of this experience should be sufficient to point to some connection between *certitude* and *arrogance*.

I would never claim that certainty makes one arrogant; that the connection exists does not mean it is necessary. There are a great many of us who live the truth faithfully while cultivating a genuine spirit of humility. Many of you, my readers (whom I have been blessed to know in real life), along with the saints and countless others furnish innumerable examples as well. St. Bernard and St. Francis, despite their profound spiritual insights, were exceptionally humble men. St. Catherine of Siena remonstrated with popes but was docile and meek. If anyone had a right to be arrogant about his knowledge it was Moses, of whom Scripture says, "the LORD would speak to Moses personally, as a man speaks to his friend" (Exod. 33:11); and yet, Scripture also says, "Moses was a man exceedingly meek above all men that dwelt upon earth" (Num. 12:3). Moses's unique knowledge of God did not make him arrogant; rather, it made him humble.

Clearly a firm grasp of the truth need not necessarily make one prideful or intransigent. But it is a common enough pitfall, nonetheless. I know this truth painfully, as I have frequently fallen into it in my own life. There is a certain perverse sort of pride that can come with knowing you are right, especially in matters of faith where one is professing the very truth revealed by God Himself. A kind of *ego contra mundum* attitude can spring up, swelling ever greater to the degree one is opposed or contradicted. It is easy to feel like we are a noble martyr for the truth when our defense is much more about being right.

And obviously it is not an either-or proposition: sometimes we really *are* defending God's truth but doing so from selfish motives or with off-putting behavior. It can be hard to tease out the dividing line when we reflect on it.

The question then, brethren, is how can we maintain a faith with such certainty that we are willing to be slain for it whilst simultaneously avoiding the vice of pride that is always liable to ensnare us? How can we be strong of faith but not obnoxiously strong-willed, arrogant, or just *annoying* when it comes to discussing it? How can we make sure we have removed the plank from our own eye before removing the speck from our brother's?

The only real answer is a continuous examination of our motives—a focus on our own spiritual life and disposition, which is really the obligation of all Christians. This is the ultimate answer. However, I have found the following specific methods helpful over the years in cultivating humility about the treasure we possess:

(1) **Resist the Temptation to view Faith in Sectarian Terms.** It is easy to treat the Faith—especially traditional Catholicism—as a sort of socio-political "movement," viewing it through a lens that is almost sectarian. Traditional Catholicism has its own media outlets, its own talking heads, its own "talking points," its own publications, partisans, and its own agenda. Not that it is wrong to have these things by any means, but it does mean we must always be on guard against treating the Faith the way we treat our own moribund secular politics. The Faith certainly has socio-political ramifications, but it is not, at its heart, a socio-political "movement," and refusing to treat it as such helps dissipate some of the hostility that comes with sectarianism.

(2) **Examen of Conscience for the Fruits of the Spirit.** St. Paul teaches us that the fruits of the Holy Spirit in our souls are nine: "But the fruit of the Spirit is love, joy, peace, patience, kindness, goodness, faithfulness, gentleness, self-control; against such there is no law" (Gal. 5:22-23). When I was a younger Catholic, I was prone to skim over passages like this and focus my attention more on meaty doctrinal verses. Not that I thought this stuff was unimportant. More like, I took it for granted that I *already possessed* these fruits and did not need to worry about it. But a soul that cannot deal with disagreement without becoming arrogant and puffed up is not demonstrating these fruits. That is why St. Paul warns that if someone is arrogant in their talk it may be a sign that they lack the power of God in their life (1 Cor. 4:18); he also warns against Christians

whose lives are characterized by "quarreling, jealousy, anger, selfishness, slander, gossip, [and] conceit" (2 Cor. 12:20). As I have gotten older, I have become more introspective about whether I possess these fruits, and more cognizant that a spirit that is joyful, patient, and gentle is not one that is habitually arrogant. Of course we must realize this is a little subjective, and there will always be those people who are wrongly accused of being arrogant *merely* because they are taking a stand for the truth. But in my experience, when a person is peaceful it is not difficult to disagree with them in a friendly manner.

(3) **Remember Faith is a Gift:** The awareness of faith as a gift is a tremendous antidote against being puffed up with pride. When we get arrogant about the truth we possess, is it not often because we view the truth as "ours?" It is easy to feel like something we discovered through our own study, our own labors, our own searching; something *we built* with our own mental and spiritual blood, sweat, and tears. We must remember, however, that *faith is a gift*. It is a gift of God in a threefold sense: (a) Divine Revelation itself is a communication from God to man, given gratuitously out of love, of truths that we would have no way of knowing by reason alone; (b) the faith we enjoy today is something that the Church of ages past delivered "once and for all to the saints" (Jude 1:3), which we receive as an inheritance; and (c) the theological virtue of faith itself is a gift bestowed on each one of us by God through baptism and maintained by grace. None of us saves himself. It is very difficult to be prideful about the certitude of faith we possess when we view it wholly as a gift.

(4) **A Lively Awareness of Grace:** What does it mean to have "eyes to see" as the Scriptures say (Ezek. 12:2)? To see with eyes of flesh is one thing, to see with eyes of the spirit is another. Spiritual sight is awareness of the movements of grace behind the scenes that form men's souls and bring

about the will of God in the affairs of men. Focusing on the working of grace helps us to decrease and Christ to increase, because we become more aware of the actions of God *behind* our affairs. Though of course we always understand the power of a good argument, we become less inclined to think, "It is my job to change this person's mind through my persuasive rhetoric," and more accustomed to see these things as in the hand of God. When we dispense divine truth, we are merely as one beggar trying to show another beggar where to find some food.

2

Mass Marketing Mysticism

🌺

In March of this year the *New York Times* published an excellent Op-Ed by Ross Douthat entitled "Mass Market Epiphany." The article concerned the way in which Americans have taken mysticism—the most interior and personal element of religious experience—and turned it into a mass market phenomenon. With clarity of insight that is unusual in the mainstream media, Douthat persuasively argues that what currently passes for mysticism in America is no substitute for true, radical mysticism; at best, it is a capitalistic, corporatized bastardization of authentic mysticism. True mysticism is intense and transcendent, while ours tends to be "a pleasant hobby rather than a transformative vocation." Perhaps I am giving this columnist too much credit for his originality; after all, he is basically repeating what Luke Timothy Johnson said in *Commonweal* in a February 2010 article called "Dry Bones" on the struggle between the exoteric and esoteric religious traditions in Christianity, Islam, and Judaism. Even so, it is refreshing to see somebody outside of the Catholic circle make this observation.

Both Douthat and Johnson accurately observe that mysticism is engaged in a "war" with what could be termed the more *exoteric* (or, activist) elements of religion—those elements centered upon the world, this life, and charitable deeds; what traditional Catholics commonly call

7

the "horizontal" approach to the Faith. It is undeniable that Christianity has been trending towards activism for several decades, even longer in the Protestant traditions. Johnson says, "Bit by bit Christianity has succumbed to the worldview of modernity, which rejects and even ridicules the notion that a life of renunciation can be a pilgrimage toward God. With the collapse of a miracle-saturated world comes the loss of a robust sense of future life counterbalancing our present 'Vale of Tears.' In the eyes of modernity, the very concept of self-renunciation appears as a form of psychopathology."

This is interesting because, despite this obvious movement away from true mysticism in Christianity (and in religion in general), polls consistently reflect that Americans consider themselves far *more* spiritual today than ever before. While only 22 percent of Americans reported having a "religious or mystical experience" in 1962, that number has jumped to 50% today. Even as numbers for church attendance drop across the spectrum, more and more Americans, many of them ex-Catholics, are describing themselves as "spiritual but not religious." How are we to understand the apparent contradiction of less and less of a connection with traditional religious piety while more and more people are describing themselves as spiritual?

The obvious answer is that people are attempting to engage with spiritualism outside of the traditional religious channels. They are pursuing the experiential element of religion without reference or context to the great traditions of the Church and the Christian mystics.

But this begs the following question: If people are seeking mystical experience apart from traditional forms of piety, how can they have any authentic mystical experience, since it is traditional religious thought that provides the framework for mysticism? Obviously, they cannot; you cannot become a Christian mystic without the structure of dogmatic Christianity standing behind the experiential. To the degree that people do pursue mysticism apart from traditional dogma, the result is a shallow, flighty esoteric veneer that not only fails as authentic mysticism, but also perverts the exoteric. Johnson says:

> In Christianity, the "new Gnosticism" espoused by devotees of labyrinths and self-realization workshops eschews the dogmas of Christianity as "underevolved." Such deracinated forms of mysticism remain oddly superficial precisely because they draw no nourishment from the great exoteric traditions...Christian mysticism that finds no center in the Eucharist or the Passion of Christ drifts into a form of self-grooming. In a paradoxical fashion, it was the exoteric frame that enabled the esoteric to dig into deep soil rather than float off into vaporous fantasy.

So the exoteric and the esoteric stand in need of each other; the latter needs the former to keep from drifting into "vaporous fantasy," while the former needs the latter to ensure that it does not become an empty formalism, a simple "plan for organizing society" with purely worldly ends.

Unfortunately, Americans have tended to do to mysticism what they have done with everything else: "democratized it, diversified it, and taken it to mass market" says Douthat in his *New York Times* piece. If you walk into any Barnes & Noble, you can go to the religious section and find books that give practical guidance on how to develop your "spirituality" and become a mystic, as if becoming a mystic was a matter of reading a book in your spare time and adopting a few surface changes to your routine rather than a life-changing *metanoia* requiring God's grace, along with the wisdom and experience that can only come from years of struggle, insight, and suffering. The mystics of the Christian tradition attained their stature by cultivating an extraordinarily rich interior life of contemplation, something that could never be taught in a single book let alone mass marketed to the general populace; even the mystical books of our saints like *Interior Castle* or the *Ascent of Mount Carmel* do not claim to be some one-size-fits-all program for those desiring to be mystics; they are rather reflective interior journals of the trials and experiences of individual souls. If general rules can be drawn from them, well and good, but the saints would have been horrified at the thought of someone using their life and experiences the way we use a Julia Child cookbook. The few books that do claim to be a general program for the spiritual life, such as the *Spiritual Exercises* of St. Ignatius, require a level of commitment and discernment that one cannot cultivate without a deep grounding in prayer and Christian orthodoxy.

Besides, as any saint would tell you, the greatest sign that one is not worthy or fit to be a mystic is strong evidence of the desire *to be one*. None of the saints wanted to have "mystical experiences;" they wanted to love God, and the experiences followed as unsought-after consolations. Furthermore, because their faith was not about having these experiences, they did not suffer loss of faith when the experiences dried up. Rather, the removal of tangible consolations served to refine and deepen their faith. Compare this to a modern yuppie, bourgeoisie "mystic" who will most likely quit any spiritual endeavor after a brief period if they don't "get anything" out of it.

Modern Christian mysticism (and by this I mean mysticism severed from tradition and discipline) is wimpy and completely divorced from its complement: asceticism. No Christian saint has attained mysticism without asceticism, yet this is precisely what modern Americans try to do: they chase mystical experience without ascesis, without mortification. Douthat says, "The closest most Americans come to real asceticism is giving up chocolate, cappuccinos or meat for lunch in Lent...by making mysticism more democratic, we've also made it more bourgeois, more comfortable, more dilettantish."

What is desperately needed today is radical renunciation. In the thirteenth century, St. Francis, appalled by the worldliness and greed of his environment, decided that the reform society and return souls to God necessitated a radical poverty that had not been practiced in the West before the rise of the Mendicant orders. Francis believed that a radical, extreme example was needed to shock thirteenth century Assisi out of its mercantile, bourgeois slumber. And his formula proved effective—effective enough to revivify the Church in Italy and across Europe and usher in the greatest period of Catholic history in Christendom.

Here is my recipe for renewal today: We need men who are willing to renounce everything and go into the wilderness, like the hermits of old. Faithful, orthodox men who, without necessarily joining a religious order or attaching themselves to a certain diocese, renounce all their possessions, wear their beards long and their hands dirty, and go out into the wilderness, eking out a penitential life of bare subsistence on isolated hillsides, in wooded freeway medians and other out-of-the-way places. These men need to be radical in their commitment to God and to renunciation. Absolutely devoted to prayer and the interior life, making a living only by begging and scavenging—a new breed of mendicants inspired by the zeal of the Desert Fathers. Their habits will be filthy, their hair disheveled, their eyes wild, and the love of God burning in their hearts. They shall be living rebukes to the materialism and activism of this age, even the activism of some of the established religious orders. When one encounters them we ought to feel like we are running into something from the Middle Ages. I say we need hundreds, if not thousands, of men to take up this kind of life. We need radical examples to remind us of what true renunciation is. It is essential for all of us to have these examples, for even our ordinary belief must in some way depend on the presence of extraordinary exemplars.

Without examples of radical renunciation, Douthat says, "Faith can become just another form of worldliness, therapeutic rather than transcendent, and shorn of any claim to stand in judgment over our everyday choices and concerns." If we can reclaim a spirit of true renunciation we will find a return to true Christian mysticism. Only then will the exoteric and the esoteric, the contemplative and the active, be harmoniously joined again for the building up of the whole Church.

3

Resisting Temptation

❧

A s long as we are in the flesh, we shall never wholly be free of temptation. The greatest saints were all sorely tempted, and our Lord Himself was tempted numerous times by the evil one as He began His public ministry. The Book of Job tells us that "The life of man upon earth is a temptation" (Job 7:1). Yet, though temptations may lead us to sin if we yield to them, they can also be of great profit when we successfully resist them. When we first swing a hammer or do a great labor on the first day of a new job, the strain of the work often wears us down. But if we perse-vere and continue, choosing to master the task rather than letting it master us, the work which wore us down at the beginning becomes easier and actually is an occasion for growing stronger. Similarly, the temptation which weakens us when we surrender to it becomes a source of strength and spiritual fitness when it is successfully resisted. But how to resist temptation?

First, we must recognize that though external factors may tempt us or exacerbate an existing temptation, we always carry about the source of temptation within us, which is illicit desire due to concupiscence:

> Every man is tempted by his own concupiscence
> [desire], being drawn away and enticed. Then when

concupiscence hath conceived, it bringeth forth sin. But sin, when it is completed, begetteth death (Jas. 1:14–15).

If we find ourselves sorely tempted by some external agent, say, an immodest poster, lewd speech, a sensual film, etc., it is prudent to remove ourselves from the source of the temptation. To be tempted is not a sin—even Christ was tempted—but to dally with the temptation and allow it to take charge of our imagination is to yield to it, and at that point what was merely an external stimulus now becomes an internal temptation, which is much more serious. Therefore, we should avoid these external agents of temptation by physically removing oneself from them if possible.

But, as James reminds us, we carry the source of temptation within us, which is our own desire. *The Imitation of Christ* teaches that while flight may save us from a particular temptation in the short term, it is not a long-term strategy for growing in virtue. The *Imitation of Christ* states:

> By flight alone we cannot overcome; but by patience and true humility we are made stronger than our enemies. He who only declines them outwardly and does not pluck out the root will profit little; nay, temptations will sooner return to him, and he will find himself in a worse condition. (I.13.iii).

Ultimately, we must learn not only to flee occasions of temptation, but to actually fight off temptation—to enter the arena with it and emerge victorious. And this *is* possible, even if the temptation seems too strong. God Himself has promised that, though we are permitted to fall into various temptations and trials, none are beyond our power of resisting:

> There hath no temptation taken you but such as is common to man: but God is faithful, who will not

suffer you to be tempted above that ye are able; but will with the temptation also make a way to escape, that ye may be able to bear it (1 Cor. 10:13).

And of course:

I can do all things through Christ which strengthens me (Phil. 4:13).

We have God's Word that we can overcome temptation—we can succeed, even if we have failed before. Why, then, do we so often fail, and how can we succeed?

There are two primary reasons we allow ourselves to be overcome by temptation: inconstancy of will and little confidence in God; conversely, the two things needed to persevere in temptation are: constancy of will and greater confidence in God.

The ability to resist temptation begins in the will. We must will to overcome the temptation. This requires the virtue of fortitude. "Jesus said to him: No man putting his hand to the plow, and looking back, is fit for the kingdom of God" (Luke 9:62). We cannot overcome temptation if we secretly harbor a desire for the sins we claim to be battling. It is necessary to have a single-minded, firm resolution to have victory. St. Augustine struggled with chastity for years, but he correctly identified that the problem with his struggle was that he had not sufficiently set his will on overcoming his incontinence, as evidenced by his famous words, "Lord give me chastity, but not yet." He recognized that he had made a truce with this sin in his heart, which caused him to have inconstancy of will when it came to overcoming it. Thus his pious resolutions came to naught.

The *Imitation* tells us:

For as a ship without a rudder is tossed to and fro by the waves, so the man who is remiss, and who quits his resolution, in many ways tempted. Fire tries iron and temptation tries the just man. We often know not what we can do; but temptation discovers what we are (I.13.iv).

It is more important to have this constancy of will at the beginning, because it is always easier to overcome a temptation when it is new than when it has already entered into the heart. It is easier to pull up a weed when it is small than after it has put down deep roots. It is easier to refuse entrance to an unwanted guest at the first knock on the door than to try to eject them after they have already entered. The longer we take in resisting, the weaker we become by allowing the evil desire to become a strong imagination, and finally blossoming into delight, then evil action of the will and sin, which brings forth death.

The second thing necessary after we have firmly set our will on resisting temptation is to have confidence in God, that He will make the grace available for your resolutions to bear fruit. "With God, all things are possible" (Matt. 19:26). Part of resolving to resist temptation is firm belief that God is able to grant us victory—that we do not fall to thinking we will always be having these particular battles. God's grace has turned greater sinners than you into greater saints—murderers, adulterers, pagans, thieves—all have found abundant grace and, in Christ, were able to persevere. This is no less true for you than for them. "But where sin abounded, grace abounded much more" (Rom. 5:20).

Therefore the two prayers that are necessary are, first, one for constancy: "Lord, help me to detest the sin sufficiently that this temptation dangles before me, such that I not only do not commit it but no longer desire it. Grant me fervency in this resolution never to entertain this temptation or commit this sin again."

Second, an act of hope in the mercy and goodness of God: "Lord, I know that in you all things are possible and that, by your grace, great sinners have become great saints. Grant me the grace to resist temptation, the confidence in the efficacy of such grace, and the vision to see myself transformed by grace, not deformed by sin."

The final principle is not to despair if we fail. God will come to our aid, even if we let ourselves down. He is quick to pardon and slow to anger, provided we are truly contrite. The important thing is not whether you have absolute success on your first endeavor, but whether you have turned your heart and are making a sincere effort. Repentance is literally translated as *metanoia*, which means "a new direction." When we repent, are we truly doing so from a desire to change our lives and start in a new direction, or is it just mere posturing? As long as our hearts are well disposed and penitent, God can work with whatever you are willing to offer Him, even in failure. "For if the readiness is there, it is acceptable according to what a person has, not according to what he does not have" (2 Cor. 8:12). In fact, when we fall is when we need to cry out to God even more, to beg for His mercy and grace. If we fall, we repent, beat our breast, confess our sins, and then take up our cross once again, confident that in Him we can and will one day reach our destination.

4

Christst Will Give You Victory

❧

This morning I did a very general confession by appointment to a very excellent diocesan priest a few towns over from me. After confession we talked for about an hour, and I had some very helpful insights that I wanted to share. None of this is novel, but even so, when it was revealed to me in the right moment it all proved to be "a word in season" (Prov. 15:23). If you are walking through a dark cloud, perhaps this will help you.

First Reflection. Do we spend too much time picking bad fruit off our tree rather than looking at the root and finding out why it is producing bad fruit in the first place? Are you confessing the same sins over and over again and beginning to doubt it will ever be different? It's good to recall that God's will for you is not to "manage" your sins; His will is for you to have total victory over them. Have you sunken into a place where you have given up hope that you will ever have victory over your sins and have begun to settle for just maintaining your current place—treading water while you try to manage your sins? This is not why Christ died for you. His death gives you the power you need to have total victory over your sins and that should be our goal and our hope.

Second Reflection. We often use a language of "distance" when speaking about our spiritual lives. Saints are "closer" to God; sin puts us "farther" from Him. However, given that

God is omnipresent, and "not far from each one of us" (Acts 17:27), we must remember that this language of distance is a metaphor for something else—it is a way of quantifying our likeness to Him; those who are more transformed by grace are "closer" to God, those who resemble Him less are "further." Really we are only ever as far from God as we put ourselves. When we sin, we can feel like God is very distant, like we are prodigals suffering in a distant land. But the truth is, there is a bit of a "Wizard of Oz" illusion; though we may feel distant, we can go home at any time if we really will to do that. The distance is only as great as we think it is. All you need to do is turn your face towards home like the prodigal son, and the father will run from the house to meet you where you are. You are home as soon as you want to be home.

Third Reflection. It's easy to reduce grace merely to a legal concept: an abstract state we are either in or out of. That certainly is part of it, but it's not the whole part. What is the point of being "in" grace? I have sometimes prioritized the mere fact of being technically, "legally" in a state of grace while ignoring the purpose of what is supposed to happen while I am in that state. Grace is not merely an indicator of whether I am in a state of friendship with God or not; it is also a vital force from God whose purpose is to work in my life to transform me. Grace is not merely adjectival ("state of grace"), but it is a noun. It is a *thing*; it is like a power or energy that is the very life of God which is lavished on us to ennoble us and enable us to love God beyond what our natural limitations would permit. What's the point of being "in a state of grace" if I am not actualizing the growth that being in such a state is supposed to make possible?

ooooo

My friend, you *can* have victory over your sins. Begin by believing this, trusting Christ to grant you this triumph, and take things one day at a time.

Even if you feel apathetic or distant from God, whether from sin or just lethargy, remember you can go home if you only will to. The distance between yourself and God is only as great as you let it be.

Don't focus only on being in a state of grace, but once there, on letting grace change the state of your life. Grace is not merely a place to be in, but a vital power God gives us to transform our lives. Be aware of its work in your life and rejoice in the small victories it wins. Christ will give you victory.

5

The Greatest Schism

❦

The title of this essay does not refer to the Greek Schism, nor to the Great Western Schism of the fifteenth century, nor even to the tremendous modernist crisis within the Church today. The schism I refer to is the unfortunate fracture between theology and ascesis, between spirituality and mortification. The more I reflect upon it, the more I am convinced that this division is at the heart of all our other problems, even the modernist crisis.

The ancient Christians referred to the Faith not primarily in terms of a set of doctrines, but as a manner of living. The earliest Christian documents call it "the Way." When Saul went to Damascus, the Book of Acts tells us his orders were that "if he found any belonging to the Way, men or women, he might bring them bound to Jerusalem" (Acts 9:2). Acts 19:9 says that at Corinth St. Paul encountered Jews who were "speaking evil of the Way before the people," and verse 23 says that "at that time there arose no little dissension about the Way." The famous ancient catechetical manual, the *Didache*, begins by announcing "there are two ways," and calls the Faith of Christ "the Way of life."

These texts all remind us that in Christianity our beliefs influence our manner of life, and our manner of life reflects our beliefs; both come together in our communal worship. This is the much commented on connection between the

23

lex orandi, lex credendi, and *lex vivendi.* All three must be united. In other words, it is not possible to have a proper comprehension of Catholic theology without participation in Catholic liturgy; likewise, attempts to enter into Catholic spirituality apart from adhering to the Church's doctrinal teaching wind up going astray, and neither our liturgical experience, our intellectual formation, nor our spiritual life can be rightly ordered if our moral lives are imbalanced. Each of the three *leges* of the Catholic faith are inalienable from the rest, as deeply united to one another as the Three Persons of the Trinity.

A beloved image of the Church from antiquity is the seamless robe of Christ; just as Christ's garment was a single piece with no seams, so the Church is indivisible. This comparison works on many levels: while it certainly applies to the Church understood in terms of her unity, it also demonstrates the interconnectedness of the different parts of the Faith, demonstrating that no one aspect of it can be compartmentalized or abstracted from the others without grave harm. G.K. Chesterton once noted that every heresy has taken some part of the truth and discarded the rest; when we stress one aspect of the Faith while neglecting others, we do violence to the seamless garment of Christ.

The schism I spoke of earlier refers to the fact that the popular icons of Catholic thought today are, by and large, divorced from any sort of regular ascetical life. Let us reflect on the lives of some of our greatest saints and doctors. We know Benedict, Aquinas, Augustine, and Bernard mainly from their writings, and that being the case, we often neglect to meditate upon the physical conditions in which they lived and how ascetical their lifestyles truly were. Benedict lived in an inaccessible cave for two years; Aquinas was a friar, in the early days when the lives of the friars still lived in true poverty and want; Bernard lived under the most severe rule then known in Europe. The lifestyle of Sts. Teresa of Avila or John of the Cross would discourage even the most ardent soul today. And let us not forget the life of St. Anthony or the other early Desert Fathers.

Yes, their lives were harsh, their penances strict, and their loneliness must have been overwhelming at times. But it was in that cave on Subiaco that Benedict first conceived his great Benedictine Rule, the masterpiece that created western civilization. It was through her fasting, vigils, and mortifications that St. Teresa received the spiritual insights that made her a Doctor of the Church; the same with John of the Cross. It was under the blazing Egyptian sun that Anthony worked out principles that are still foundational in Christian spirituality. Aquinas was austere in his personal life, went about barefoot, lived his life in drab, clammy cells that most of us could not tolerate for a weekend, and died prematurely, wasted away by a life of penitence and asceticism. But it was in the midst of this ascetical regimen that the intellect of Aquinas was flooded with the divine light that graced the Church with the *Summa*. To put it bluntly, the saints can talk the talk because they walk the walk.

Ah, but what can we say of our modern spiritual writers? In what crucible of mortification were our current spiritual writers formed? Not a drizzly cave or a scorching desert or atop a pillar, but in a cozy little diocesan institute of higher learning. Their authority comes not from sleepless nights of anguished prayer, bodies wracked from fasting or feet calloused from walking this earth unshod, but because they have obtained a certificate from a diocesan-approved two-year program that says they are "qualified" to be a spiritual director! At night they go home, not to a drab monastic cell to catch a few hours of sleep on a stiff board, but to a suburban home somewhere to enjoy all the comforts of modernity.

And what of our theologians? Do they walk the earth barefoot? Do they abstain from meat for six months out of the year, as did the early Franciscans of which St. Bonaventure, one of the Church's greatest theologians, was a member? Do they die prematurely because of the rigors of their penance? Alas, no.

Our modern spiritual thinkers have talked the talk, but they have not walked the walk, at least not in the manner that it was walked by the saints.

The result is a tremendous divorce between theology and asceticism that chokes up the channels of grace. This means that our theology and spirituality become more man-centered, more a product of human reason and human feeling than divine truths and spiritual light. I realize I am being vague here, and that it is difficult to generalize—and that people will think, "How do *you* know what so-and-so does in his private life?" My friends, I do not know what so-and-so does privately, nor how much he fasts—but I know that *most* of our theologians and spiritual writers today are not living anything close to what even the simplest monk or priest would have endured a millennium ago. I understand there will be exceptions, but overall, I suspect this thesis is correct. In the past, we had theology and spirituality that proceeded from a life of faith lived out in all its rigor; today, it is largely the domain of "experts" whose approach is extremely anthropocentric, because it is book-learned, based on the latest theories, and the product of unaided human reason.

Ah, Lord, send us holy monks, holy hermits, holy nuns—men and women whose capability to speak on these matters proceeds from a life that is crucified and hidden with Christ, which is something that cannot be earned with any certificate program or degree. Who will reconnect our spiritual life with our intellectual life? Who can refasten the chain that once held the sun to the earth? Who can repair this schism?

6

Mortification and Penance

✤

In my essay, "The Greatest Schism," I posited the theory that one reason we have so much bad theology today is because theological studies in the West are divorced from any sort of regimented ascetical discipline. This means the faith becomes something that is solely academic, robbed of its living power. St. Paul said that his preaching was so efficacious because it was "not in the persuasiveness of the words of philosophy, but in the demonstration of the Spirit and power" (1 Cor. 2:4), meaning that his preaching did not flow simply from learning, but from a life lived in Christ. Mortification is necessary for the Christian life.

To be sure, proper intellectual formation is important, but unless theology is coupled with a life lived as a pleasing sacrifice to God, it is always missing something, lacking in a certain depth. The theory I posited in the aforementioned essay was that this deprivation is particularly profound in the modern world, and that this lack means our teaching is more likely to go astray, because it is this ascetic spirituality that develops the spiritual "intuition," which recognizes the voice of Christ and helps keep one away from false teachings. This is what St. John the Apostle meant when he said:

> And as for you, let the anointing, which you have received from him, abide in you. And you have no

27

need that any man teach you; but as his anointing teaches you of all things, and is truth, and is no lie. And as it hath taught you, abide in him" (1 John 2:27).

It seems, unfortunately, that my argument here has been misunderstood, specifically from the folks who made comments such as, "But you don't need to do severe penance to be holy," offering St. Thérèse's Little Way as an alternative; others questioned the whole need to do penance ("Can someone tell me why we need to flay ourselves alive every day to procure grace?"), suggesting that the simple sufferings of a broken home or a struggling marriage are sufficient mortifications.

A few further clarifications are therefore justified: First, we need to make a distinction between "mortification" and "severe penance," or "flaying ourselves alive" as some would have it. Mortification simply consists in self-denial. This can take a variety of forms and need not be severe; in fact, as many pointed out in the combox, most mortifications ought not be severe. To mortify simply means to "put to death." What we put to death is our flesh, and we do this through self-denial. Every single Christian, *without exception*, is called to practice mortification. This is why St. Paul says of himself, "I chastise my body, and bring it into subjection: lest perhaps, when I have preached to others, I myself should become a castaway" (1 Cor. 9:27); and he encourages this on every believer when he says, "For if you live according to the flesh, you shall die: but if by the Spirit you mortify the deeds of the flesh, you shall live" (Rom. 8:13) and "Mortify therefore your members which are upon the earth; fornication, uncleanness, lust, evil concupiscence, and covetousness, which is the service of idols" (Col. 3:5). Mortification is obligatory on every Christian.

How this mortification looks will vary depending on

our station in life and degree of spiritual maturity, and there are as many ways to practice self-denial as there are circumstances in life. So we must understand that mortification does not equate to severe penance in most cases. We are right to say we need not all do severe penance, but we err if we infer thereby that mortification is not necessary.

Second, let us recall that in the context of my original essay, I was speaking of the ideal *for theologians* to live lives of mortification, since there is a profound connection between what is understood in the intellect and what is experienced in the spiritual life. The two reinforce each other, and without a sound grounding in each, the other tends to lose its moorings and can drift; spirituality devoid of intellectual formation becomes sentimentalism, emotionalism, and ultimately pantheism, while a merely intellectual faith without any spiritual growth becomes sterile and eventually open to novelty. Humility of thought and mortification in life keep everything in proper balance and result in a theology that is sound, balanced, and vivified by grace, such as the works of Aquinas, Augustine, Bernard, and the other great saints. To the degree our theology has gone wrong, I am convinced this is a very real cause.

As for the question of whether simply enduring suffering is itself a mortification, the answer is yes and no. All the saints agree that patiently enduring tribulation and offering it to God is the most pleasing form of mortification and results in an abundant growth in spiritual strength. However, it is not mere suffering, but suffering endured *patiently* and *offered to God*. There is no merit in suffering for the sake of suffering; it is a tool, and it depends upon what one does with it. Furthermore, we might add with St. Paul that Christian Tradition presumes this suffering is only meritorious if it is unmerited. Our first Pope phrases it this way:

> For this is thankworthy, if a man for conscience toward God endure grief, suffering wrongfully. For what glory is it, if, when ye be buffeted for your faults, ye shall take it patiently? but if, when ye do well, and suffer for it, ye take it patiently, this is acceptable with God...But let none of you suffer as a murderer, or a thief, or a railer, or a coveter of other men's things. (1 Pet. 2:19–20, 4:15)

Simply growing up in a broken home, or living in poverty, or enduring a tragedy or some kind of abuse does not mean the suffering has been meritorious. It *can* be if it is handled rightly, but the mere fact of suffering is not meritorious. And even if these things have been suffered, the call to mortification is constant; we can never say, "I have denied myself enough in the past, I need not do it anymore." It would be just as silly to say, "I have exercised enough last year; I do not need to do it this year." *Ascesis*, after all, means "training" in Greek.

Let all Christians practice mortification in whatever manner is appropriate to their state in life and level of spiritual maturity, subject to the approval of their confessor. Let Catholic theologians bind their academic life to a spiritual discipline of prayer, fasting, and penance that their doctrine may be pure and their teaching pleasing to our God and Lord Jesus Christ.

Let us conclude with the words of the great Dutch mystic and spiritual master, Thomas à Kempis:

> What is the reason, why some of the Saints were so perfect and contemplative? Because they labored to mortify themselves wholly to all earthly desires; and therefore they could with their whole heart fix themselves upon God, and be free for holy retirement. We are too much led by our passions, and too solicitous for transitory things. We also

seldom overcome any one vice perfectly, and are not inflamed with a fervent desire to grow better every day; and therefore we remain cold and lukewarm" (Chapter 11).

7

God Loves You

✤

appy Easter! Rather than write for friends today, I
have decided to deviate from the usual routine and
write for those who may have stumbled upon this essay
accidentally: you who are sitting around this Easter with
anxious hearts wondering whether you should become a
Christian—or, if you already are a Christian, evaluating
why you should hang on to your tottering faith.

Yes, tottering faith. There are many obstacles to faith in
today's world. Modern reductive science conditioning us to
think that to understand a thing is simply to explain what it
is made out of; the world full of unspeakable evils at home
and abroad, all of which challenge our confidence in an
all-good God; temptations of the world—pleasure, wealth,
and the good opinion of men—all of which make a Christian life seem fraught with difficulty; finally, the scandal
frequently offered by those who bear the name of Christ yet
fall far short of Christ's call, serving as painful reminders of
the sinfulness of us all.

Yes, there are many obstacles. But an obstacle is not an
impossibility. "Nothing shall be impossible with God" (Luke
1:37). God can overcome all, even death. Even your faltering
faith. Ask Him. Ask Him for the gift of faith. And then be
humble enough to receive it when it was given, knowing that
it is often given in seed form—just a very small measure,

which must be nourished and protected before it can grow up into a mighty tree.

Why do we need God? We all fall short, my friend. All of us have messed up, despite our best intentions. We might not all have killed someone; we might not all have committed adultery, but we have all really fouled things up. No matter what we wish, we tend to choose selfishly. That is part of our nature. The world has told us that if we just tweak a little here, offer some more programs there, that we can build a material utopia. Well, even when the will and the means are there, human nature tends towards selfishness. It's just the way it is.

Not that our nature is bad. It is from God. People are good. But not perfect. We are flawed. Christians call this original sin: the fact that, while we are basically oriented to the good, we are unable to carry it out because there is also a streak of selfishness within all of us. Our whole race is fallen. This is why attempts to fall back on human ingenuity and materialist ideologies to build a better world are doomed to fail.

But God did not leave us in this darkness. When the time was right, He sent His only Son to take flesh and become a man. Jesus Christ took on human nature in its fullness. He felt the sweat of a hard day's work, endured the drudgery of human life, saw the world in all its frailty. But He did not succumb to its evil; though a man like us, He never committed or experienced sin, because He was also fully divine. Coming from God, He was fully God; in becoming man, He was fully man. Both God and Man—a Godman, and as such, the only one capable of reconciling man and God.

He came to earth in obscurity, lived a perfect life, and then suffered the humiliating death of crucifixion, though He was innocent. In giving Himself to the very last, He showed Himself utterly selfless and thus undid the selfishness of mankind; because He was divine, the love with which He carried out this act of self-sacrifice was so eminently pleasing to God that it wiped away the debt of sin that separated man from God. Just as God and Man come together in the Person of Christ, so God and Man are brought into harmony by the death of Christ.

And because that death was so perfect, that love so fulsome, that sacrifice so perfect, death could not keep Him chained. Yes, He rose from the dead, for "love is stronger than death" (Song of Solomon 8:6). This Resurrection was a vindication—a vindication of His teaching, but also of His identity. He manifested Himself to His disciples, who bore witness that Christ was truly risen from the dead.

And how does this effect you, dear friend? You see, Christ rose not just for Himself but on behalf of the whole human race. In Him, God has elevated and ennobled human nature. His death merited glory for Himself, but grace for all. He rose to glory, yes, but He makes possible *your* rise to glory as well. His Resurrection makes possible newness of life for you through His grace. Freedom from your sins. Freedom from your past. Freedom from whatever characterization you or others have created for yourself. Free from your passions which enslave you. Free to live as a son of God.

Yes, this is all for you. He died for all mankind, but He also died for you individually: because He created you, because He loves you. Yes, God loves you. I know it's cliche, but it is true. But don't let that truth be an occasion for apathy. The idea that the God of the Universe loves you is no cause for laziness or sloth; if He loves, He expects something from you, just we all do of those whom we love. "Doesn't God love me right where I am? Why does He demand I change?" Oh yes, God loves you right where you are—but He loves you too much to leave you in that condition.

What holds you back? There will always be objections, questions, uncertainties. Faith is a knowing, but it is also a kind of darkness. Faith does not depend on a mass of probabilities or on whether you have every detail worked out. Faith comes down to this: Do you or do you not believe that Jesus Christ rose from the dead? If He did, then He is who He says He is and everything else follows. If He did not, the whole Christian faith is in vain. Yes, vain.

What is your answer to the question? Did He rise from the dead?

And if so, if you know down in your heart that it is true, then rejoice! You have the gift of faith, the seed of eternal life. Do not let it die. Nourish it. Nourish it in the truth. When our Lord rose, He did not leave us orphans, but sent the Holy Spirit among the Church that He founded, thus promising to lead it into all truth, so that though He is no longer on the earth according to the flesh, the Spirit of Christ can forever lead the brethren of Christ in the true Church of Christ; and this is that Church of which Peter was given the keys and made head.

Yes, there will be scandal. Yes, there will be embarrassment due to human error, arrogance, and sin. But ultimately it is irrelevant to your own faith. Did Jesus rise or didn't He? He rose in power; that is what this day commemorates. And if you hold close to Him, you have power too. Power to remake the world according to God's law, starting with yourself, then the Church, then the world. It doesn't matter what *they* do; *you* keep doing what *you* know you need to do. If the Church needs holiness, *you* be holy. If the world needs compassion, *you* be compassionate. If you do not see Christians devoted to prayer, *you* be devoted to prayer. The kingdom is within you, and it starts with you. Heaven begins in your heart today.

You have questions? So did I. But there are answers. There will be time for that. Many, many people have walked this path before you and there is no difficulty that has not been considered and resolved.

So believe the Gospel. Repent of your sins and resolve by the help of God's grace to put them away forever. Live in the freedom of the children of God. Drink the pure milk of Christ from the Church which Christ endowed with His Spirit. Frequent the sacraments. Pray intensively and make the acquaintance of other prayerful people. Honor the Church. Love God above all, as He has loved you. Make no compromise with the world. Do these things and you will experience the power of Christ's Resurrection. And the joy and freedom you will possess in Christ now is but a foretaste of the eternal reward your faith will bring you in Christ, who brings all things to fulfillment.

But what if you do not yet have faith? Then pray for it. God will grant it if you are sincere in following Him. That is really all it takes is an assent of mind and will to follow God and put Him above all. He will bring it to completion.

Amen and amen! He is Risen indeed!

8

Good, Acceptable, and Perfect Will of God

*

Do not imitate this world, but be transformed by the renovation of your minds, and you shall distinguish what is the good, acceptable and perfect will of God (Rom. 12:12).

Our holy faith teaches that there are unequal degrees of beatitude in heaven. Session 6 of the Council of Florence taught that those in heaven "clearly behold the triune God as he is, yet one person more perfectly than another according to the difference of their merits." Everyone is blessed in heaven, but their degrees of blessedness differ.

This inequality of eternal beatitude is due to the inequality in merit from soul to soul. Some souls fulfill the will of God in a near perfect manner, conforming themselves most intimately to Christ, and by doing so, merit much glory; others, like the workers called at the end of the day in the parable of our Lord (cf. Matt. 20:1–16), are received into heaven, as it were, by the skin of their teeth. Each group will be saved, some close to perfect when they die, others only after enduring the purifying fires of Purgatory to various degrees.

Heaven receives those who toil ceaselessly for the Lord bearing the long hours and the heat of the day, as well as those who were only called in the last moment of their lives, and many in between. There are different ways of fulfilling the will of God, with varying degrees of perfection. There is a manner of fulfilling God's will that is perfect, another way that is less than perfect but still truly good and meritorious, and then a lesser way that is merely acceptable. While everybody strives to fulfill the will of God in the manner most consistent with his state and manner of life—and remembering that "if the readiness is there, it is acceptable according to what one has, not according to what he lacks" (2 Cor. 8:12)—it is nevertheless true that certain forms of life and devotion are objectively better than others. This has long been understood in the case of virginity, for example, which the Catechism says is a "more intimate" way of following Christ, most appropriate for "pursuing the perfection of charity" (CCC 916).

In the passage from St. Paul cited above, the great Apostle speaks of a will of God that is good, acceptable, and perfect; that is, a manner of following God that approaches evangelical perfection, a lesser way that is still "good" but not perfect, and finally, a way that is merely "acceptable" or tolerable. This parallels our Lord's teaching that whilst obeying the commandments of God (i.e. avoiding mortal sin) will secure eternal life, there is another, higher way to follow Christ for those who "would be perfect" (Matt. 19:21): the traditional evangelical counsels. Those who observe the evangelical counsels are living an objectively "better" life than those who do not.

The Church Fathers also taught different degrees of perfection based on one's manner of following God. A common text that lent credence to this idea was Mark 4:8 and Matthew 13:8, the parable of the sower, in which our Lord speaks of good seed, which "brought forth fruit that grew up, and increased and yielded, one thirty, another sixty, and another a hundred-fold" (Mark 4:8).

Following our Blessed Lord's interpretation, the Church Fathers identified the different yields with different manners of life. The martyrs are those who produce a hundred-fold increase; the sixty-fold increase is assigned to the virgins, and the lowest yield, that of thirty-fold, is assigned to the faithful who remain in the married state. For example, St. Cyprian, when writing to consecrated virgins of the Carthaginian church, invoked the parable to remind them of the spiritual yield their state in life will produce: "The first fruit for the martyrs is a hundred-fold; the second is yours, sixty-fold" (*On the Dress of Virgins*, 21). The same parable was interpreted in exactly the same manner by Augustine (*On Holy Virginity*, 46), St. Jerome (Letter 68:2), and Origen (*Exhortation to Martyrdom*, 14).

St. Paul says that we must run our race so as to win (1 Cor. 9:24). Paul often compared the Christian life to an athletic competition. In any athletic competition, competitors will be ranked from first to last—but even so, each is expected to give their all. If a runner does not strive to run as fast and hard as he can, how can he be said to be running so as to win? Although not everybody will place the same, the essential characteristic of a competition is that one tries their hardest. First place is the goal in every athlete's mind; if it were not, how could they be realistically running "so as to win?"

To relate this back to the passage from Romans, we should all be striving to do God's "perfect" will, not just be content with what is merely "acceptable." Does this sound daunting? In our own strength we could never hope to do this, but our Lord does not command what is impossible. In grace such a life of perfection is truly possible. The saints are those who have attained it.

There are various practices that Catholic tradition has hallowed as being a sure means towards attaining holiness. St. Bernard and St. Alphonsus both compiled famous lists or "steps" that would lead to holiness: fasting, devotion to our Lady, Holy Hours, regular and devoted attendance at Mass, obedience to superiors, acts of penance, and many other things also lead us towards holiness. All are forms of mortification, that is, ways by which we "put to death" the deeds of the flesh so we can live in the spirit (cf. Rom. 8:13).

But mortification, by its very nature, is difficult. But it is necessary. This is why St. Paul says of himself, "I chastise my body, and bring it into subjection: lest perhaps, when I have preached to others, I myself should become a castaway" (1 Cor. 9:27); and he encourages this on every believer when he says, "For if you live according to the flesh, you shall die: but if by the Spirit you mortify the deeds of the flesh, you shall live" (Rom. 8:13). And, "Mortify therefore your members which are upon the earth; fornication, uncleanness, lust, evil concupiscence, and covetousness, which is the service of idols" (Col. 3:5). Mortification is obligatory on every Christian.

The Christian who is perfectly mortified has attained perfection, because to be perfectly mortified means to be dead to this world and fully alive and set apart to God. Unfortunately, people are often led into thinking this perfection is available without too much effort. Popular Catholic books promise to help readers "unlock the power of the sacraments;" pamphlets for Holy Hour devotions boast that they can quickly teach you "five ways to tap into the Eucharist;" books are published with collections of excerpts from the spiritual writings of the saints which are put forward as a streamlined, "what-you-need-to-know" guide to Catholic spirituality. Our spirituality, like our society, has become bourgeois.

These aids may be good to orient one in the right direction, but we fool ourselves if we think holiness is gained easily. The much-touted universal call to holiness means that holiness is possible for everybody, not just religious.

But it does not mean that holiness is easy or that it is less rigorous to attain for the lay person than the contemplative. There is no "lay version" of holiness that is effortless or can be reached with some self-help books in a few quick and easy steps.

There are different degrees of penance and different types of mortification, but all must do penance; all must be mortified. All things being equal, holiness is easier to attain in the religious life than the lay state. Yes, there will always be holy lay people and lax religious, and the former will be higher in heaven than the latter. But this is due to a defect in the observance of the religious; in other words, while a faithful lay person can attain a higher degree of holiness than a bad contemplative, a faithful contemplative will attain a higher degree of holiness than a faithful lay person, simply because his manner of life is more conducive to mortification and holiness.

Does this offend you, reader? Does it upset you to think that some levels of holiness will not be open to you because of your state in life? Yet it is true: Martha and Mary both do good, but Mary has chosen the better part. Certainly, even us Marthas can cultivate a bit of Mary, but it is impossible that we should simultaneously receive the reward of Mary while living the life of a Martha.

There are always temptations to think that we can attain holiness without fundamentally mortifying our flesh or changing our manner of life. This is simply not the case. Yes, we may make great strides; we may move from what is merely acceptable to something better. But if we seek perfection—as we should—the way is always going to be difficult and will always involve great struggle. This is why common patristic symbols for the spiritual life all involve *struggle*: an athletic race, wrestling, a battle, climbing a mountain, etc.

There is a way to follow God that is merely acceptable, one that is better, and one that is perfect. A real path to holiness should involve moving from one to the next. A false path to holiness is one that will look simply to affirm what you are already doing, or that would seek to pretend that holiness can be attained without any serious effort. What is good for one may not be good for others; for a great sinner, merely getting him to stop blaspheming daily may be a considerable advance. But for a mature Christian seeking holiness, such a bar is set far too low. In that case, the good can become the enemy of the best.

Let us ask ourselves, "What would my life look like if I were seeking to fulfill the perfect will of God? What would I look like as a saint?" We cannot imitate the great penances of the Desert Fathers in the lay state but let us not deceive ourselves: there is room for much more effort than we practice. What does this look like for a lay person?

Begin by asking: do we seek to fulfill our state in life perfectly, or only tolerably? Are we eager to latch on to mitigations, exceptions, and exemptions in our obligations, or do we make sacrifices by voluntarily renouncing these things as a means of challenging ourselves? Are the only times we fast on Ash Wednesday and Good Friday? Have we kept Advent penitential? Are we mortified in the use of our finances? How about in our sexual appetites? In what other ways do we "buffet our bodies to bring them into submission," as St. Paul says? Do we structure our daily routine around prayer and the service of God, or do we assume this is impossible and give God merely what is left over? If we were really to—I mean *really*—live our state in life faithfully and not just tolerably, what would it look like?

Again, we need not intimidate ourselves by thinking that penance necessitates severe austerities, but we are fooling ourselves if we think it does not require mortification. Let us reexamine our life. Are we deluding ourselves into thinking we are mortified when really we are living a manner of life that is merely "acceptable" and not really "good," much less "perfect?" Remember, the biggest enemy of the best can be the good. We cannot imitate the religious life perfectly, but those who seek perfection, of whatever state, will approximate to the evangelical counsels as closely as they can. Society has changed, but the definition of holiness has not changed; neither have the steps to get there.

One final quote from a saint who is not often associated with austere penances but who was exceptionally mortified: St. Elizabeth Ann Seton. Here is a prayer composed by St. Elizabeth as an act of abandonment to the divine will in all matters, even the most trivial:

> Considering the infirmity and corrupt nature which would overpower the spirit of grace, and the enormity of the offense to which the least indulgence of them would lead me—in the anguish of my soul, shuddering to offend my adored Lord, I have this day solemnly engaged that, through the strength of His Holy Spirit, I will not again expose [my] corrupt and infirm nature to the smallest temptation I can avoid; and, therefore…I will make a daily sacrifice of every wish, even the most innocent, lest they should betray me to deviation from the solemn and sacred vow I have now made (Fr. Joseph Dirvin, CM., *Mrs. Seton*, 113).

This is the prayer of a saint who sought perfection, not just what was "acceptable." The universal call to holiness means we are all capable, with great efforts done in grace, of attaining some degree of holiness: too often it is taken to mean that we are already basically holy. Instead of making the world holy, it has made holiness worldly. We ought to be exceptions to this. We know the acts of true piety, and the Church's tradition presumes they are objectively standardized, and that those who do them in the right disposition will be holier than those who don't.

Let us, then, follow the path that has been blazed for us, and begin by resolving to follow God's will perfectly in a spirit of humility and penitence. The way is not easy but putting our souls under the discipline will render the yoke easy and the burden light. Let us have great confidence in our Lord to complete the good work He has begun in us (Phil. 1:6) and remember that "I can do all things through Christ who strengthens me" (Phil. 4:13).

9

Study on to Salvation†

❦

Praying, fasting, and almsgiving, the three eminent
good works. Blessed is the man that studies to perfect
these three parts of his Christian life. Those ten and strict
commandments, blessed is the man who keeps these perfectly
and who has the love of the Father and the company of our
Lord constantly (cf. John 14:23).

It is interesting to note how many great Saints were illit-
erate and yet so perfect in virtue and full of wisdom. For
example, St. Anthony of the Desert never learned how to
read or write, and yet he came to a great understanding of
virtue through its constant practice and imitation of those
around him who exceeded him in virtue.

It seems to have become like an echo that continues to
reverberate throughout the Catholic world in recent times
"Know your faith" or "We have to study our faith." In my
limited experience of going about to Catholic gatherings or
listening to recordings of various conferences and homilies,
it is normally one of the primary solutions presented to the
crisis in the Church proposed to the faithful.

The exhortation to come to know one's faith is a good
one. Faith most certainly comes from hearing (Rom. 10:17),
and all scripture is useful for teaching (2 Tim 3:16:17). But

---

† Written by dom Noah Moerbeek, CPMO.

just like prayers can be said out of self-love or out of a desire to be seen, fasting for vanity, and almsgiving for human respect, study of the faith can become an occasion for curiosity, a source of pride, a distraction from duty, a departure from the cross. Like any good thing, it must be subjected to reason, and it must have some specific end in mind.

But what does the great Thomas à Kempis advise? "Leave curious questions. Study such matters as bring thee sorrow for sin rather than amusement." (*The Imitation of Christ*, Chapter 20) It is fair to say that it does a man no good to memorize all the scriptures or have an encyclopedic knowledge of the Catechism when he offends God by his life by breaking the commandments. We shall know if our study is motivated from the desire to please God if it is done with the mind of conquering sin, growing in virtue, the defense of His honor, or the perfecting of a good work.

If you feel irritation at me because you believe such a thing is obvious, let me explain why I mentioned it. Ever know a Catholic apologist who could not guard his tongue from bad speech? How about Catholic bloggers who cannot help themselves at slandering and attacking others? Or knowing a person who, after studying theology, feels more comfortable in committing sins because they better understand the distinctions between mortal and venial sins? (This is explicitly mentioned as a problem in *Outlines for Asceticism for Seminarians* by F. J. Remeler, a pre-Vatican II textbook).

I'm sure you could think of your own examples. The truth is that the world, the flesh, and the devil will do anything to interfere with the keeping and perfecting of the commandments and of our own prayer, fasting, and almsgiving. God, in order to confound His enemy, allows us to be tested, like He did with St. Anthony; but He is present during the struggle of his faithful. "The Lord is as a man of war; Almighty is His Name" (Exod. 15:3). St. Anthony of the Desert said, "Let this especially be the common aim of all, neither to give way having once begun, nor to faint in trouble, nor to say: We have lived in the discipline a long time: but rather as though making a beginning daily let us increase our earnestness."

Whenever we pick a work to study, hear a homily, or observe virtuous actions, let us strive to make practical resolutions to become more pleasing to God, especially by more strictly keeping the commandments and perfecting good works. By doing this, God Himself will teach you, "And as for you, let the unction, which you have received from Him, abide in you. And you have no need that any man teach you; but as His unction teacheth you of all things, and is truth, and is no lie. And as it hath taught you, abide in Him" (1 John 2:27).

No matter what one does—apologetics, teaching catechism, instructing home-schooled children, or just being a good neighbor—this is the means of study that gives glory to God's kingdom and draws others to Christ our King. The great Fr. Garrigou-Lagrange said in his master-piece, *The Three Conversions of the Spiritual Life*, that "[the interior life] is important to us not only as individuals, but also in our social relations; for it is evident that we can exert no real or profound influence upon our fellow-men unless we live a truly interior life ourselves."

So let us not run to study to find excuses to break commandments, avoiding dry prayer, enduring hunger, and or suffering deprivation. But, as St. Anthony said, "Let us daily abide firm in our discipline, knowing that if we are careless for a single day the Lord will not pardon us, for the sake of the past, but will be wrath against us for our neglect."

10

Hearts of Stone to Hearts of Flesh

❧

These days we hear an awful lot about Catholics leaving the Church. It seems every time we go online we read that some Catholic friend or another is going through some crisis of faith or has abandoned the practice of their religion altogether. But though the Church's demographic crisis is undeniable, there is also a steady stream of conversions to the Church. They come from all walks of life to seek salvation in the barque of Peter: they come from Protestantism, from New Age mysticism, from atheism, or sometimes they move from lax, non-practicing Catholicism back to the observance of the Gospel. Some come just because a path of study and prayer leads them, but others come in under circumstances that are fascinating. Often the story of their road to Rome is filled with so much coincidence that it is hard to see it as anything other than providential.

In this essay I will share five of my most beloved stories about people brought into the Faith through the most unexpected means. In each case I have given only the most abbreviated accounts: no doubt there were more steps, more people, more moments of grace involved, but I think I have presented the crux of each story accurately. These stories are all taken from the lives of acquaintances I know personally.

The Wrong Priest

An agnostic young man with a sordid history and nothing but ridicule for the Catholic Church took a dare from a friend to go into a Catholic confessional. He stopped randomly at a parish in Detroit and went into the confessional with the intention of mocking the priest and wasting his time. Little did the man know he had walked into the confessional of Fr. Eduard Perrone of Assumption Grotto, one of the wisest and most beloved priests in the Archdiocese of Detroit and definitely the wrong priest to pick on casually. The priest asked, "What do you have to confess?" The man arrogantly said, "Nothing." Father Perrone said, "We'll see about that." He took out an examination of conscience pamphlet and started reading through it, asking the man whether he'd committed each sin. By the end of the list the man had broken down and realized his sinfulness. He made a sincere repentance and was received into full communion with the Church not long after. He later became a catechist in his own parish.

Converted by Beauty

A man and his fiancé were driving through the country. They were secularists, both fallen-away Catholics. They were planning on getting married later that year and were on the lookout for a church—any church—that "looked pretty" so they could be wed somewhere scenic. They saw a small little Catholic Church off the main road and pulled off to check it out. It was a beautiful neo-gothic structure that had somehow survived the wreckovation of the 1970s, retaining its 19th century high altar and most of its art. The pastor happened to be in the church and greeted the couple. They told him they wanted to get married there "because the church is so pretty." The pastor delivered a catechesis on what the Church is, why the art is so beautiful, what it all represents. By the end of the meeting, the two signed up for

RCIA. They returned to the practice of the Faith and were married in the Church later that year.

Just One Traditional Latin Mass

A young man who was quite a way through medical school was invited to Mass by a priest who regularly says the Traditional Latin Mass. He was uncertain about Catholicism in general, let alone the Traditional Latin Mass. The priest implored him. "Just come to one Latin Mass," he told the student. The young man assented and attended the one Traditional Mass. He was blown away by the beauty of what he saw. A year later he was in the seminary. He has now been a priest for over fifteen years. Just one Traditional Latin Mass. The priest who told me this story stated that he had personally led over ten men into the priesthood in a similar manner.

For Love of France

A young man from Flint, Michigan (frequently rated the most dangerous city in America) had a powerful conversion to non-denominational, Protestant Christianity. He never felt completely at home in any church, however, and tried to fill the void by getting involved in a lot of ministries, mission trips, etc. Eventually he wound up on a Protestant "mission trip," not to the Third World, but to France, where his church intended to convert secular Catholics to their form of non-denominational Protestantism. Whenever he had spare time, he would sneak away and sit in the various little parish churches scattered throughout France, many dating to the Baroque era or older. He fell in love with French culture, taught himself French, and, realizing that the most essential thing about French culture was Catholicism, began exploring the Church. He was received into full communion this past fall on the Feast of Christ the King and is currently discerning whether he may have a vocation.

Beautiful Singing

An ardent atheist who had made a very determined rejection of God and His Church had a Catholic wife. She attended Mass alone for many years and prayed patiently for her husband. Eventually the husband consented to come to Mass with his wife, where he was struck by the beautiful singing of one of the cantors. The beauty of the singing melted his resistance, and he became convinced of the reality of God. His heart being softened by God's grace, his intellectual opposition withered away. Not long after he entered RCIA and was received into the Catholic Church the following Easter. The cantor served as his sponsor.

You will note that in none of the above cases was the person converted by hearing a bunch of arguments. It was other things: beauty, liturgy, a sense of their own sinfulness, the glory of Catholic culture. To be sure, after their hearts were converted, argumentation and intellectual reasoning stepped in to solidify them in their faith, but in none of these cases did rational argumentation precipitate their conversion. This is certainly not to say that nobody is ever "argued" into the faith; many people are. But how God chooses to bring individuals into the Church are as varied as people themselves.

These stories should give us confidence in the power of God's grace. He calls whom He wills. It is *His* Church and He can bring in anybody through any means He chooses. When we see something like this unfolding before our eyes, our job is to support these people with prayer and, when necessary, by answering their questions. But *we* do not make converts, at least not in the strict sense. The Holy Spirit, "who convicts the world of sin, of righteousness, and of judgment" (John 16:8), it is He who makes converts by turning hearts of stone to hearts of flesh (cf. Ezek. 36:26). Faith is a gift.

11

Eat Dung, Get Sick

❧

Whatsoever things are true, whatsoever modest, whatsoever just, whatsoever holy, whatsoever lovely, whatsoever of good fame, if there be any virtue, if any praise of discipline, think on these things (Phil. 4:8).

The Christian life calls us to vigilance against the works of darkness and the wiles of the evil one. Too much filth has been unleashed in the Church to afford anymore negligence, naivete, or head-in-the-sand Pollyanna-ism.

This, however, must be balanced by an equal, if not greater, focus on wholesome things; as St. Paul says, our thoughts should be turned towards the true, the modest, the just, the holy, the lovely, the virtuous. We are to be children of light (cf. Eph. 5:8), and our minds should be turned towards the light. The things St. Paul proposes for our meditation are subjects that ennoble us; they elevate our intellect, shaping it according to the designs of God. Elsewhere, Paul tells us that part of faith is having a "resurrected" mindset; if we have been resurrected with Christ, our minds, also, ought to be raised: "Therefore, if you be risen with Christ, seek the things that are above; where Christ is sitting at the right hand of God; mind the things that are above, not the things that are upon the earth" (Col. 3:1–2).

To do otherwise is to damage our faith. We can only

focus on the works of darkness so much before the shadow falls over us, as well. In the *Lord of the Rings*, Saruman was corrupted by looking through the Palantir. He did so at first only to gain intelligence about Sauron, to be educated about the enemy's activities; but eventually it bent his mind towards darkness, causing his fall.

Consider now what media you consume, whether secular or Catholic. Is it always focused on exposing some evil somewhere? Is it ever dwelling on the deeds of malicious agents? Is it scandal-mongering, ever purporting to be doing the necessary dirty-work of chronicling the train of abuses and perverse deviations of the modern Church? There is certainly a place for this sort of reporting, but does the media outlet exist only to peddle scandal? And is this *all* you consume? Is this the entirety of your spiritual diet?

While it is important to be "wise as serpents" about the goings-on in the Church and world, existing primarily on this sort of diet is harmful in the long run. Like Saruman gazing into the Palantir, it warps your ability to see things properly—to see things as God would have us to see. It can make us skeptical, jaded, and cynical, ultimately causing our love to grow cold. The epistle from the Traditional Latin Mass today tells us, "Be ye of one mind, having compassion one of another, being lovers of the brotherhood" (1 Pet. 3:8). The brotherhood, of course, is the Church. Do you love the brotherhood? Do you love the Church? That is, when you think of the Catholic Church—not as you wish it to be in some golden past, but as it actually exists today—is it an object of desire? Is it something attractive that moves the will? Despite the problems, despite the warts and sores, do you possess a deep and abiding affection for your first love?

I am not naïve about the Church; I know that the Church does a lot to push people away. It seems today to be undergoing some kind of catastrophe, and seeing it is like watching helplessly while one's own mother goes through an embarrassing midlife crisis. I do not suggest the Church isn't culpable for a great many things. But, that being the case, why on earth would you want the scope of your vision darkened further by drinking more deeply of the sludge? Yes, the air is poisoned; but the poisoned air means that we must build up our immunities that much more. To do anything else is to gamble with our faith.

Remember, people who lose faith don't just stop believing. They stop *loving*. Then, their love having grown cold, the hope that keeps them anchored unravels, and hope being dissolved, faith dies. This is why St. Paul urges us to meditate on that which is good and pure and wholesome. It is the spiritual equivalent to eating a balanced, healthy diet. But if you eat dung day in and day out, don't be surprised if you get sick.

12

Personal Relationship
with Jesus

❧

"Do you have a personal relationship with Jesus?" Ah, how fond I was of this question when I was going through my Protestant phase as a young man! It was an excellent way to trip up unprepared Catholics. "Yes, you profess belief in God, but do you have a *personal* relationship with Jesus?" Chances are a poorly catechized Catholic would not know how to respond, and stumbling, would at least momentarily reconsider their standing before God.

A good Catholic should of course realize that this is a canard; *all* practicing Catholics have a relationship with Jesus; what do you think happens when we receive Holy Communion anyway? Just because we do not share the same vocabulary as Protestants does not mean that we do not possess the reality of which they speak. We ought never to let non-Catholics trip us up and get us thinking that we don't have a relationship with Jesus because we don't adopt their terminology to explain our spiritual experiences.

As a Catholic, it has been a long while since I have heard this phrase bandied about. And even though no thinking Catholic should be taken aback by this phrase, it is good to revisit this now and then to remind ourselves—and Protestants—that, yes, Catholics do have a "personal relationship with Jesus." In fact, this friendship with Christ is the source of the spiritual life so recommended to us by all the Church's great contemplatives.

There are many places we could go to establish the point, but let us take an excerpt from the famous *Imitation of Christ* of Thomas á Kempis. I choose this work because it was written during that awful 15th century, the century before Luther when (allegedly) the corruption of the Catholic Church was at its height, an era of ignorance when Catholic spirituality was (allegedly) both superficial and superstitious. This book is not only a classic on Catholic spirituality, but an excellent place to refer Protestants who suggest that the Catholic religion dissuades one from having a personal friendship with Christ our Lord. Kempis writes:

On The Intimate Friendship of Jesus (Book 2, Chapter 8)

WHEN Jesus is near, all is well and nothing seems difficult. When He is absent, all is hard. When Jesus does not speak within, all other comfort is empty, but if He says only a word, it brings great consolation. Did not Mary Magdalen rise at once from her weeping when Martha said to her: "The Master is come, and calleth for thee"? Happy is the hour when Jesus calls one from tears to joy of spirit. How dry and hard you are without Jesus! How foolish and vain if you desire anything but Him! Is it not a greater loss than losing the whole world? For what, without Jesus, can the world give you? Life without Him is a relentless hell, but living with Him is a sweet paradise.

If Jesus be with you, no enemy can harm you. He who finds Jesus finds a rare treasure, indeed, a good above every good, whereas he who loses Him loses more than the whole world. The man who lives without Jesus is the poorest of the poor, whereas no one is so rich as the man who lives in His grace. It is a great art to know how to converse with Jesus, and great wisdom to know how to keep Him. Be humble and peaceful, and Jesus will be with you. Be devout and calm, and He will remain with you. You may quickly drive Him away and lose His grace, if you turn back to the outside world. And, if you drive Him away and lose Him, to whom will you go and whom will you then seek as a friend? You cannot live well without a friend, and if Jesus be not your friend above all else, you will be very sad and desolate. Thus, you are acting foolishly if you trust or rejoice in any other. Choose the opposition of the whole world rather than offend Jesus.

Of all those who are dear to you, let Him be your special love. Let all things be loved for the sake of Jesus, but Jesus for His own sake. Jesus Christ must be loved alone with a special love for He alone, of all friends, is good and faithful. For Him and in Him you must love friends and foes alike, and pray to Him that all may know and love Him. Never desire special praise or love, for that belongs to God alone Who has no equal. Never wish that anyone's affection be centered in you, nor let yourself be taken up with the love of anyone, but let Jesus be in you and in every good man. Be pure and free within, unentangled with any creature. You must bring to God a clean and open heart if you wish to attend and see how sweet the Lord is.

Truly you will never attain this happiness unless His grace prepares you and draws you on so that you may forsake all things to be united with Him alone. When the grace of God comes to a man he can do all things, but when it leaves him he becomes poor and weak, abandoned, as it were, to affliction. Yet, in this condition he should not become dejected or despair. On the contrary, he should calmly await the will of God and bear whatever befalls him in praise of Jesus Christ, for after winter comes summer, after night, the day, and after the storm, a great calm.

This idea is at the center of the Catholic mystical tradition; every saint, mystic, and contemplative had a rich "friendship" with our Lord Jesus Christ. The old catechisms often defined being in a state of grace as being in a "state of friendship" with God. The most profound manifestation of this friendship is the devout reception of our Lord in Holy Communion, where Christ entrusts Himself to us and we receive Him in an act of love. It is a communion of love and friendship in the truest possible sense.

This is not to say that our communion with Christ is equivalent to the "friendship" touted by Protestants. Catholic friendship with Jesus Christ does not become cheapened by a crass, base familiarity (or at least it should not). Jesus is truly our friend, savior, intercessor, and companion; but He is also Lord, God, King of Kings, He who will break the nations with a rod of iron (Ps. 2). Thus, our friendship with Him must never lose sight of our true stature in relation to Him; we draw near to Him, but with awe, and without giving in to the kind of sappy emotionalism ubiquitous in modern worship music, where people sing about Jesus as if He is their boyfriend. Our friendship is characterized by an affectionate devotion, devoid of the language of over-familiarity that does not adequately communicate God's majesty.

"Wherefore, my dearly beloved...with fear and trembling work out your salvation" (Phil. 2:12).

13

Discouragement from Habitual Sin

❧

Do you struggle with discouragement from habitual sin? For many Catholics, this is a huge problem. There is a pattern we tend to fall into: we do well for a while, but when faced with temptation we give in and sin. The sin brings apathy, a sense of, "Well, I already blew it, what's the use in trying?" So you go into a slump—your prayer life suffers, you keep committing the same sin over again (because you already messed up, so what does it matter?), and you get apathetic. Maybe a week goes by. Maybe a month. You feel like a slob, spiritually and in other respects. Eventually you are so unhappy and angry with your life that you rouse yourself; you say, "I have to get right with God." You go to confession and lay your soul bare before a confessor. He gives you some good advice, you repent tearfully, receive absolution, and go out rejoicing, resolved to do better this time. You are grateful for God's mercy and kindness at giving you another shot, and things go well for you spiritually. Things continue this way for a time—maybe a few weeks, maybe a few months—until you get complacent, get tempted, and fall again. Then the cycle repeats. Year after year after year. Maybe decade after decade.

This can be frustrating in the short term, but the long

term consequences are more dire. Repetition of this pattern over many years can lead us down a dark path, the steps of which include:

+ *Acedia* (spiritual sloth): "It's inevitable I'm going to commit serious sin sooner or later so there's no point trying to make spiritual progress."
+ *Distraction*: Unhealthy focus or preoccupation with just "that one sin" such that you ignore other important aspects of your spiritual life.
+ *Resentment*: Simmering bitterness towards God. "It is unfair of God to prohibit something I am unable to restrain myself from doing. It puts me in an impossible position."
+ *Blindness*: Inability to see the working of grace in one's own life.
+ *Dulling of Conscience*: Once having accepted the inevitability of certain sins, the conscience dulls to them; we get used to that sin or at least to the idea of living with the sin.
+ *More Time Outside of Grace*: The lengths of time we perceive ourselves to be in a state of mortal sin grow longer and longer; the times we are disposed to receive Communion grow shorter and fewer, until they are like small islands of grace in a vast sea of sin.
+ *Loss of charity*: A gradual hardening of heart takes over. We become jaded and angry, impatient with ourselves and others. The very ideas of spiritual progress, grace, etc. seem like jokes.
+ *Loss of Hope*: "At the rate this is going, it will be a miracle if I make Purgatory."
+ *Despair*: "How can I—or anyone—possibly avoid being damned to hell? The vast majority of us are simply doomed."
+ *Loss of Faith*: You no longer perceive the issue as your

problem, but as a problem with the faith itself. "The Catholic religion doesn't work. It only gives me stress and anxiety. This system simply *can't* be the truth. I can no longer assent to this."

Discouragement at habitual sin can thus create a slow decline that ultimately leads to loss of faith. It is good to recall that Satan is in this for the long haul. While individual sins certainly matter, the devil is aiming bigger than that; he is trying to create an overall trajectory in our life that leads us away from God. He is attacking us strategically, while we tend to get bogged down in the bushes, unable to see the forest for the trees.

Do you recognize this pattern in your life? Even if you are not to the point of despair or loss of faith, does any of this sound familiar? It very well may. I've been here for sure. And so have many Catholics, for whom the pattern above is the reality of their spiritual life. Not all will eventually lose faith, of course; people spiral down this vortex to varying degrees. But many of us have been (or are on) this path *somewhere*.

What is the way to get out of this spiral? The real problem is that "Try harder next time" and like advice doesn't seem to help. Most have been struggling every way we know how to free ourselves from habitual sin for *years*. Some eventually have victory; many don't. Is there a better way?

We ultimately need to reframe how we look at this problem, and it starts with revisiting the idea of "winning" and "losing" against temptation. When we are tempted, we are thrown into a spiritual battle, a battle we can either win or lose. But *when* do we win or lose—at what point is a particular spiritual conflict *won*, or conversely, at what point is it *lost*? Most of us will answer that the battle is won when we pass on without committing the sin, and that it is lost if we commit the sin with which we are struggling. How many of us, after fighting with a temptation, fail to persevere and then think, "Well, I lost that battle," or something similar?

While it is true that victory over temptation is a "win," it does not follow that committing the sin is a "loss," at least in a certain sense. Consider this: thinking "I lost that battle" implies that the spiritual battle is over once you have committed the sin. Nothing could be further from the truth. What happens *after* we sin is just as important. The battle isn't just whether you will sin; it is how you will respond to the victory or failure. If you have victory, will you become complacent and idle? If you are defeated, will you become discouraged, fall into a slump, and go down the slope described above? The battle *after* the sin is pivotal, as it determines whether you will be solidified in a certain spiritual trajectory.

Therefore, when you commit a habitual sin, rather than thinking, "I've lost again," or "I blew it," or "There's no point in praying or trying now that I'm already in a state of sin," instead think, "The battle is not over. I am moving into a new stage of the battle. I can still have a tactical victory here." Even if you have sinned, your prayers still matter. God is still just as invested in helping you. You don't need to throw in the towel. You don't need to beat yourself up; focusing excessively on your own failures is itself a trap meant to paralyze us. The battle has not ended; I can have victory at any time if I choose God now *in this moment*. The moment of grace was not at some place in the past when you were struggling between light and darkness; the moment of grace is *now*; it is always now. All you have to do is strike *now* and you win. Every time. The victories will be varied. The journey will be bumpy. But you'll get to where you want to go. Where you are heading is more important than whether the road you are on has potholes. It's not so much whether you hit potholes; it's whether the potholes eventually cause you to give up and turn around.

Maybe this is nothing new. I am certainly not promising

any breakthroughs. But I am sharing something that has been extremely helpful in my own spiritual life—realizing that the battle does not end if I sin, that the moment of grace is now, and that as long as I seek God in any given moment I always win; these have proven to be transformational principles. Perhaps they will be of some help to you as well.

Happy Advent, brethren.

14

The Hidden Work of Grace

❧

When I read the testimonies of those who have lost faith or had their faith severely shaken, I frequently notice these persons will mention the imperceptibility of grace as an issue. Usually commenting on the uncharity of other Catholics, they will say things like, "The operation of grace does not seem present in the Catholics I know; if we are the true Faith, shouldn't it be more noticeable?" or, "I don't see the effects of grace in their life."

What this ultimately comes down to is people aren't as good as we expect they should be. Even though it is cliché, it is not an empty argument. After all, the essential trait of a Christian is supposed to be that we are "Christ-like," which supposes the sanctification of the person through the working of grace. And this is not an abstract principle—it is supposed to bear fruit in all manner of tangible signs: fruits of the spirit (Gal. 5:22–23), corporal works of mercy (Jas. 1:27), and the development of virtue. This is all made possible by grace. If grace is real, shouldn't we clearly notice these manifestations of it?

Furthermore, when Christians fail to respond with grace in sensitive situations, it stings. It stings hard. Too often Christians—who should be the most reassuring—respond with coldness or astonishing hubris. I seldom speak of my own life on here, but I want to share some of my own experiences in this regard: I am a divorced Catholic and have been so for several years. When this happened, I received virtually no support from my Catholic friends whatsoever. I am not talking about institutional support from the Church; I'm talking about Catholic friends reaching out and saying, "Hey, how are you doing?" Or saying, "Want to go out and do something?" Nobody started a sign-up to bring me any dinners. Invitations to social events dropped off; I stopped getting invited to weddings. They quietly stopped interacting with me online. Even my kids stopped getting invited on play dates and such things. People stopped chit-chatting with me after Mass or at Sunday coffee and donuts. It's not that people were expressing outright judgment towards me; it's just that they weren't...*anything*. It was so disappointing. I ended up having to make a whole new set of Catholic friends.

Ironically, guess who was right there for me? My secular or non-Catholic friends. They wanted to take me out to soothe my wounds. They texted me, "Hey how are you feeling?" They were right there to say, "Aw, life happens, man, I'm sorry." They did good to me without any expectation or sense of obligation. May God reward them. But feeling abandoned by my Catholic social circle was devastating. To be honest, I'm still kind of angry about it. I pray for peace! And I don't understand it. Did they think that by simply being my friend through a hard time they were supporting the concept of divorce? If so, that's ridiculous; that would be like saying I can't visit someone in prison lest it be construed I support his crimes. It was extremely hurtful to see that the persons whom I believed ought to have been the most charitable and grace-filled were being outpaced by non-believers. It was my most painful experience with Catholics I ever had, and it wasn't with the clergy or institution, but with the rank-and-file schlubs in the pews who I thought were my friends.

Shouldn't these people—who receive the Body of Christ weekly or even daily—have responded with more grace to my pain?

As I've reflected on this over the years, I've come to see it this way: people generally do the best that they can with the knowledge and gifts they have available to them. It is easy for me to say, "If you *really* had grace, you should have done X or Y in a given situation." But neither I nor anyone can evaluate a person's objective state on the spectrum of grace. Perhaps someone's behavior to me was a little off-putting; I don't know how much worse it would have been without grace. Maybe someone is a braggart and has always been a braggart for the last ten years you've known them, and despite all their communions and prayers, they are the same bragging fool as they've always been. Well, thank God they are the same bragging fool and not a *worse* one! That, too, is grace. Perhaps so-and-so comes to Mass dutifully every week, says little, contributes little, understands little, and makes little progress. But how do you know that simply maintaining this station does not require everything he has? Is not the meaning of the widow's mite parable that it's hard to judge the true value of a person's progress on mere externals?

Life is hard; even with grace it is still a struggle. God knows I have let people down, too. I have had friends call me in need, and I blew them off because their need was inconvenient to me at the time. I've looked the other way. I've sinned by omission. I've been arrogant. But that doesn't mean grace hasn't been working in my life. When I look at where I've come from and where I am now, my entire life is a miracle of grace. I know I have a long way to go still, but that's just because I am a work in progress, and "it hath not yet appeared what we shall be" (1 John 3:2). But this is ultimately a journey; we are all pilgrims. If I am walking from Detroit to Los Angeles, the fact that I have not arrived at Los Angeles is no argument that I never left Detroit. A traveler must not only consider where he needs to go but how far he has come. So it is with grace. And thus I have come to the conclusion that it's impossible for me to judge how and to what degree grace works in peoples' lives. I simply don't know where people are on their individual journeys. I rejoice when I see moments of grace, but I cannot use these moments to make any sort of judgment on a person's overall state.

Of course, it is rare for someone to become truly saintly. We all know where we want to be: fruits of the spirit, works of mercy, virtue, etc. But few people progress in the spiritual life to the point where these things become resplendent; few reach sanctity this side of heaven. Think about something like physical exercise. Of all the persons who say, "This year, I'm going to get in shape!", how many of them do you think actually persevere in that resolution? How many of them are actually in shape by next year? The minority. Some make nominal gains, then give up. Many exert considerable effort merely to maintain the status quo. Only a few make demonstrable progress that is noticeable by others. Given that the spiritual life is compared to athletic training, requiring similar endurance and discipline, should we be surprised that so few become exceptional?

There certainly are many circumstances when grace is discernible. In my own life I can discern many places where grace has worked me over the years and brought about real, substantial change. Is this the sort of change others can easily see from the outside? Not necessarily. Again, others don't know what I struggle with, just like I don't know what others struggle with. Sometimes we have victory in one area and continue to fight elsewhere. I am infinitely more patient and loving now than I was 15 years ago. That's grace. But I also have failures, sins, and bad habits I continue to struggle with. I may be more patient now, but I am just as much of a blabbermouth as I was 15 years ago. It's grace that I am not worse. Someone may easily discern I am an inveterate blabbermouth, but they may not discern that I am more patient or loving. Thus, anyone who would presume to judge the work of grace in my life based on the former without knowledge of the latter would be horridly mistaken in their judgment.

All of us have similar stories of grace to tell. And in many cases it is discernible in their life, but only after one has really gotten to know them, entered into their world, and understood where they are coming from. Grace, after all, works like a "still, small voice;" it is engendered by the Spirit, which "blows where it wills, and you hear the sound of it, but you do not know whence it comes or whither it goes" (1 Kings 19:12; John 3:8). It is always working. And when we complain that we don't see it, we are merely complaining that it does not work the way we think it should work, bearing the fruit we think it should bear, visible in the manner we think we should see it, in the times and circumstances we believe it should be seen.

Instead of looking about at the Church and saying, "Grace doesn't seem to be working in these peoples' lives," actually sit down with these people and say, "Brother, tell me a story of how grace has been working in your life," and you'll hear an astonishing tale almost every single time. I am willing to believe it will be more interesting and edifying than whatever *you* assumed grace ought to be doing. After His Resurrection, the disciples asked Christ, "Lord, will you at this time restore the kingdom to Israel?" (Acts 1:6). Imagine the disappointment of those who could not let go of their own conception of what Christ's work ought to be! But for those who let go of their own expectations of what should be and instead received what Christ actually wanted to give, how rich their joy must have been!

Ultimately, we must avoid trying to judge where and

how grace is working in the lives of others, and especially avoid sitting in judgment over how we think it *should* be working. That is a recipe for frustration and impatience with others—loss of charity, loss of hope, and ultimately loss of faith. Christ's teachings, "Judge not lest ye be judged" and, "Remove the plank from your own eye before removing the speck from your brother's eye" are not just platitudes to help us be nice; they are life-giving principles that keep us humble, grounded, and seeing the way God sees. And once we see with His wisdom, the works of grace become manifest.

15

The Spirit of Lent

✤

I have heard it on good authority from Muslims that during Ramadan, when Muslims are expected to fast from sunrise to sunset, it is not uncommon for there to be lavish feasts and parties thrown after sunset that are grander in scope than any festivities outside Ramadan. In this way, the technical obligation of fasting during Ramadan is observed, but the penitential nature of the season is obfuscated.

A similar phenomenon can and does happen with Catholics during Lent. Not wanting to be too burdened down with the obligations to do penance that Lent imposes, we find little ways around them—ways to still be festive and at ease in the midst of the Church's most intense period of penance; ways in which we fulfill the letter of the law whilst completely missing the purpose of this season of austerity.

The examples are legion, but I think you know what I am talking about. Here are some common Lenten loopholes:

+ Staying up until midnight feasting the day before Ash Wednesday and Good Friday so you don't experience hunger the next day.
+ Conversely, staying up until 12:01 on Ash Wednesday or Good Friday and pigging out on meat as soon as the fast is technically over.
+ On fast days, eating one massive, grossly inflated meal

so that your "two snacks" that can't equal the size of the meal can likewise be larger than usual—in practice, two other meals.

+ Going out of the way to create Friday meatless meals that are nevertheless lavish, extravagant, or excessively celebratory, as if Fridays in Lent are not meant for penance but rather for an exercise in culinary creativity.

+ Changing your Lenten resolutions midway through Lent or applying them on different days to get around enforcing them (YOU: "I'm giving up movies for Lent!" FRIEND: "Hey, wanna go watch a movie this Tuesday?" YOU: "Uh...well, that's cool because I'm only giving it up on Mondays, Wednesdays, and Fridays!")

I wave no finger of judgement; I would not list any of these practices if I had not been guilty of them myself. And I say not that they are necessarily prohibited (though they are probably venially sinful). And the Church does allow us considerable leeway in our Lenten penances. These habits do, however, evidence a lackadaisical attitude towards Lent that views the season in terms of the *bare minimum*. When we focus on the bare minimum, it becomes possible for us, too, to miss the spirit of the season, even if you are not guilty of these more egregious examples.

Whatever your Lenten regimen, the point is that Lent is supposed to be penitential. What does it mean for a season to be penitential? It does not simply mean that we notice Father is wearing purple, give up meat for a few Fridays, cover our mouths jokingly when we almost say "Alleluia," or patronize the parish Fish Fry. Penance has an objective element (hence the Church's Lenten disciplines that are binding on everyone), but it is also a profoundly personal and subjective thing. When the Church tells us that a season is supposed to be penitential, it means nothing other than that we are supposed to *experience* it as penitential. If we intentionally arrange our circumstances in such a way as to avoid experiencing any unpleasantness, difficulty, or challenge during Lent, then we are entirely negating the purpose of the season.

How can we do this? This depends upon the circumstances of your household. Many Catholic households observe meatless Fridays all the time, not only during Lent. Beyond that, even though Friday meals are always meatless, these families also try to make them simple, frugal affairs that lack flair and ostentation. Broccoli and rice. Tomato soup and grilled cheese. Baked beans and mac n' cheese with dinner rolls and water to drink. These families understand that we are supposed to *feel* and realize that we are being deprived of something, not manipulate our circumstances to offset the penitence of Lent by creating little islands of pleasure within the season over and above what we would being doing under normal circumstances.

If we are going to go through the trouble of observing Lent, we want it to be of real benefit to our souls. There is a threefold way to do this:

In the first place, *use Lent as an opportunity to cut off a bad or sinful habit* that you ought to be giving up anyway. There are graces available to those who avail themselves of the penance the Church prescribes for this season, with real opportunities for growth in holiness. We ought always to be striving to cut off sin, but Lent is an especially appropriate time to do this.

Besides this, *give up something that is a legitimate good*, and something that is actually challenging (in other words, something you will experience as penitential). There is benefit to our souls in depriving our bodies of a legitimate good, because they help unshackle the reason from the passions and redirect it towards heavenly ends. Even so, remember that a smaller penance done with great regularity and devotion is better than an extreme penance done in fits and only now and then.

Finally, add an *extra devotion to your life*: extra periods of prayer, extra visits to the Blessed Sacrament, more daily Masses if possible, extra Scripture reading: something that can help dispose the soul more towards God during this time and take advantage of the grace God offers us. People often miss the connection that part of the purpose in giving up an activity during Lent is to replace it with prayer. If we are giving up watching movies, then the time we would have spent doing that should be at least partially spent in some activity conducive to the salvation of our souls, not some other fun activity that replaces the one we are giving up. If we usually watch a movie every Thursday afternoon, but during Lent we go to the indoor waterpark on that day instead, then we are missing it. If we gave up chocolate, we do not gain anything by eating Skittles in its place. Offer up the longing for chocolate you experience as a prayer for the sanctification of your soul.

Lent ought to be experienced as penitential. If not, we are wasting our time. This is a big problem in the Church today; Catholics know penance only by name, only as a sacrament, or perhaps a season that is said to be "penitential," but we do not know penance as St. Paul did: "I chastise my body and bring it into subjection." Why? "Lest perhaps, when I have preached to others, I myself should become a castaway" (1 Cor. 9:27).

16

The Art of Fasting

❧

No ascetic discipline is so universally recommended by Scripture and Tradition as the practice of fasting. And, paradoxically, no practice is so universally neglected in modern Catholicism. From the tales of Abraham to the fasting of the Ninevites, who averted the wrath of God by their penance, to the tale of Sarah who fasted before her wedding to Tobias, to the words of our Lord that certain demons could only be overcome by fasting, Scripture is replete with examples of the importance of fasting and its efficacy in purifying the soul and obtaining God's favor; the lives of the saints afford us with thousands more examples.

But how necessary is fasting to the advancement of the spiritual life, and what fruits do we derive from the practice? Let us examine these questions in light of Tradition, Scripture, and the teaching of St. Robert Bellarmine.

It is first necessary to establish whether fasting is a precept or a counsel for Christians. Of course we are not speaking of those days of fast and abstinence that are mandated by Canon Law, but rather the practice of fasting as a form of spiritual asceticism. Is this sort of fasting a practice that is merely counseled, similar to celibacy, or is it a precept, such that it is such a necessity of the spiritual life that those who do not do it may gravely endanger their soul?

It is an interesting fact of Christian history that the

earliest of the Church Fathers are more interested in telling Christians when they should *not* fast than mandating when they should. For example, the *Didache* instructs Christians to avoid fasting on the same day as the Jews so as to avoid being lumped in with "the hypocrites:"

> Your fasts should not coincide with those of the hypocrites. They fast on Mondays and Tuesdays; you should fast on Wednesdays and Fridays (*Didache*, 8).

Thus, the earliest teaching on when Christians should fast is determined by way of negation. But in ruling out certain days of the week, the *Didache* does in fact imply that Christians are *expected* to fast. This early tradition lived on in the practice of observing fasting during the Ember Days, which are the Wednesday, Friday, and Saturday after the First Sunday of Lent for spring, after Pentecost Sunday for summer, after the Feast of the Exaltation of the Cross (14th September) for autumn, and after the Third Sunday of Advent for winter. The implication in such days being set aside for fasting is that Christians will fast.

Our Lord Himself implied the same thing, and like the *Didache*, did so in the context of contrasting Christian fasting with the fasting of the Pharisees:

> Moreover, when you fast, do not be like the hypocrites, with a sad countenance. For they disfigure their faces that they may appear to men to be fasting. Assuredly, I say to you, they have their reward. But you, when you fast, anoint your head and wash your face, so that you do not appear to men to be fasting, but to your Father who is in the secret place; and your Father who sees in secret will reward you openly (Matt. 6:16, 18).

Our Lord's attitude is one of presumption; He simply takes

it for granted that Christians will fast, and not thinking it necessary to establish this point, He goes right on to discuss the manner in which Christians ought to fast. This suggests fasting is meant to be normative for the Christian life.

Given the attitude of our Lord, the words of the *Didache*, and other Christian writings on the subject (all of which presume fasting) and all of the examples of fasting afforded us by the Old and New Testaments and the lives of the saints, it seems safe to say that fasting is a necessary part of the spiritual life for any serious Christian; no Christian who avoids fasting is serious about his or her spiritual life.

Yet, it seems also that we must stop short of stating that fasting is a morally binding precept, in such a way that those who fail to fast beyond the prescribed times are guilty of a specific sin or will be damned for not fasting (and remember, we are speaking about fasting *above and beyond* the times of fasting prescribed by the Church, which most certainly are precepts). Thus, it can be said that fasting is a necessity, but only a *general* necessity, not a *strict* necessity. It is a necessity in the same way that reading the Scriptures is necessary; certainly, anyone who wants to get to heaven and advance in their spiritual life will read the Scriptures, for "ignorance of Scripture is ignorance of Christ," as the Catechism says—and those who positively refuse to read the Scripture most likely endanger their soul. Even so, one could not say that reading the Bible is necessary for salvation in the strict sense, since people can go to heaven who have not or cannot read the Scriptures. Fasting seems to be in this general category; it is not strictly necessary, but you jeopardize the resilience of your soul against sin and temptation if you positively refuse to fast. So, for all practical purposes, fasting is a necessity for any serious Christian.

But why is it so necessary? The reason fasting is so necessary is because its fruits are so manifold that it becomes an indispensable aid on the journey to sanctity.

St. John Chrysostom summarizes the importance of fasting quite succinctly when he says, "Fasting is the support of our soul: it gives us wings to ascend on high, and to enjoy the highest contemplation" (St. John Chrysostom, Homily 1 on Genesis).

St. Robert Bellarmine also encouraged fasting. Let us look at the five fruits of fasting, according to St. Robert Bellarmine in his *Art of Dying Well:*[1]

1) **Fasting Disposes the Soul for Prayer:** In order to pray effectively, one must set the mind on things heavenly and pull our attentions and affections away from things merely earthly, which drag our minds and hearts down and serve as a barrier to contemplating divine things. Fasting aids us in detaching our attention from things temporal and disposes us to more effectually commune with God. Hence, Moses fasted for forty days in preparation for his communication with God on Mount Sinai (Deut. 9:18); Elijah similarly fasted for forty days, and Daniel fasted for three weeks before receiving the series of visions that comprise the second half of the Book of Daniel (1 Kings 19:18, Dan. 10:2–3). Likewise our Lord fasted for forty days as He prepared Himself for his mission, and St. Francis of Assisi spent a month in prayer prior to receiving the holy stigmata. In the Church's liturgy, great feasts are traditionally preceded by periods of fasting, for it is evident from the examples of the Scriptures and the lives of the saints that we are better disposed to pray effectually when in a state of fasting.

2) **Fasting Tames the Flesh:** St. Paul admonishes us to "crucify the flesh, with its vices and concupiscences" (Gal. 5:24) and offers himself as an example, saying, "I chastise my body, and bring it into subjection" (1 Cor. 9:24). While the body is certainly not evil as the Manicheans taught, it

---

[1]   St. Robert Bellarmine, *The Art of Dying Well* (Sophia Institute Press: Manchester, NH, 2005), 57–64.

nevertheless can become a distraction in the service of God because of the many bodily urges and passions that attempt to bend our will towards gratifying them. There are many bodily desires, but perhaps the most primal and fundamental bodily desire is the desire to eat. Hunger is experienced by all persons of both sexes, of all ages and all states in life. It is the fundamental bodily urge and is most indicative of our creaturely state and our contingent existence—it is the king of all bodily desires. Therefore, when we by fasting dethrone this king and force the urges of hunger to submit to the will, we progress greatly in taming the flesh and subjecting it to our reason. There is no means of subjecting the flesh that is more effectual than fasting.

3) **Fasting Honors God:** Besides this, fasting also gives honor and glory to God. This is because we ourselves, trained by asceticism, become living sacrifices that are pleasing to God (Rom. 12:1) This is why the Council of Nicaea, in Canon 5 calls the Lenten fast "a clean and solemn gift, offered by the Church to God." Pope St. Leo the Great also calls fasting a sacrifice: "For the sure reception of all its fruits, the sacrifice of abstinence is most worthily offered to God, the giver of them all" (*Second Sermon on the Advent Fast*). Therefore, fasting is a sacrifice that gives honor and glory to God.

4) **Fasting is Penitential:** Fasting is also a means of atoning for the punishment due to sin. This is related to what was said above regarding hunger as the king of the bodily desires. Because we are in the flesh, we all need food for nourishment, and thus the practice of fasting becomes inherently unpleasant; to effectively fast is to truly crucify the flesh, and though we can accustom ourselves to the practices, fasting itself is something that is difficult, unpleasant, and requires virtue to do consistently. Thus, it becomes an act of penance, which we can offer to God in satisfaction for the penalty due to sins. The Scriptures and the Fathers

give us many examples of this. The anger of God was averted by the fasting of the people of Nineveh, and the Jews in the days of Esther appeased God by prayer and fasting. Many citations from the Fathers could also be offered in support of this teaching but let us offer only two: St. Cyprian of Carthage admonishes his people, "Let us appease the anger of an offended God by fasting and weeping, as He admonishes us" (*On the Lapsed*, 29). St. Augustine also says, "No one fasts for human praise, but for the pardon of his sins" (Sermon 60).

5) **Fasting is Meritorious with God:** Finally, fasting is meritorious with God, both in the sense that it is effective in obtaining favors from God, and in that fasting itself merits a divine reward. Hannah fasted and her prayers were heard by God because of her fasting, and she thus conceived the prophet Samuel; similarly, Sarah was delivered from a demon after fasting for three days. Our Lord warns us that certain demons can only be overcome with fasting (Mark 9:29) If we return to the passage from the Gospel of Matthew cited above, we note that our Lord promises a reward for those who fast:

> But you, when you fast, anoint your head and wash your face, so that you do not appear to men to be fasting, but to your Father who is in the secret place; and your Father who sees in secret will reward you openly (Matt. 6:17–18).

So fasting assists us in obtaining God's assistance in our temporal affairs and also merits an eternal reward.

Now that we have examined the necessity of fasting and the fruits we derive from the practice, let us look at the manner in which we ought to fast, taking chiefly as our guides the words of the prophet Isaiah and the teaching of St. Robert.

In the book of the prophet Isaiah, the Israelites complain

that, despite fasting in accordance with God's proscriptions, their prayers are not heard and they seemingly derive no benefit from their fasting. They say, "Why do we fast, and you do not see it? Afflict ourselves, and you take no note of it? (Isa. 58:3). In the following verses, God warns them that their fasts are unacceptable for a multitude of reasons. Let us look at His response:

> Lo, on your fast day you carry out your own pursuits, and drive all your laborers. Yes, your fast ends in quarreling and fighting, striking with wicked claw. Would that today you might fast so as to make your voice heard on high! Is this the manner of fasting I wish, of keeping a day of penance: That a man bow his head like a reed, and lie in sackcloth and ashes? Do you call this a fast, a day acceptable to the LORD? This, rather, is the fasting that I wish: releasing those bound unjustly, untying the thongs of the yoke; setting free the oppressed, breaking every yoke; sharing your bread with the hungry, sheltering the oppressed and the homeless; clothing the naked when you see them, and not turning your back on your own (Isa. 58:4–7).

In the first place, though food is given up, God notes that they have not given up quarreling and fighting. The lesson is that the purpose of fasting is to mortify the flesh. The flesh cannot be mortified if it is denied in one manner but gratified in three others. The practice of fasting must go hand in hand with a general disposition of humility and penitence that accompanies all our actions, even those not strictly related to our fast. St. Robert Bellarmine says the same thing:

> Nor do they derive any fruit who, although they may eat more moderately, yet on fasting days, do not abstain from games, parties, quarrels, dissensions,

lascivious songs, and immoderate laughter: and what is still worse, commit the same crimes as they would on ordinary days (*The Art of Dying Well*, 64).

God also chastises the Jews for the same reason our Lord does: they bend the head and lie in sackcloth and ashes so that it may be readily apparent to all that they are fasting. But what is true fasting? God says it ought to be an occasion for doing works of charity, clothing the naked, setting free the oppressed, etc., and what's more, our Lord adds that this ought to be done with a clean appearance and fresh countenance, so it is not readily apparent that we are fasting.

The Church proposes fasting for us during the period of Lent, before certain great Feasts, during the Embertides, and during Advent. But this is all of a very nominal sort: two snacks and one meal not larger than the two snacks. Yet the example of the saints was much greater: many, like St. Francis, spent up to a third or a half of the year in periods of fasting. Even if our occupations or state in life do not make such radical practices possible, most of us could stand to fast a little more. After looking at all of the benefits we derive from it, what excuse could we possibly have not to?

17

The Rosary and Poverty†

❧

"I have no silver and gold, but such as I have give I thee" (Acts 3:6). These are the great words of our first Pope, St. Peter, when someone asked him for alms while he was going into the temple to pray. Of course, what happened next was a miracle: in the Name of Jesus Christ, St. Peter gave the man the ability to walk.

There is a great deal of talk today about social justice, but if anyone out there is talking about patience in poverty, I have not heard it. There is a great deal of talk over what governments should do with their citizens' money, but little talk of the need for penitents to give alms for the forgiveness of sins. It feels sometimes as if some were saying "I have no silver and gold, but what I do I have I give you, in the name of social justice, you should get benefits."

Today the politics of envy and greed abound. This development is not surprising; in fact, it was predicted by our Holy Father Pope Leo XIII of holy memory in his encyclical *Laetitiae Sanctae*: an encyclical on how the Rosary is a great remedy to the evils afflicting society.

Let us look at what Pope Leo identified as one of those three evils. He begins by saying:

---

† Written by dom Noah Moerbeek, CPMO

> There are three influences which appear to Us to have the chief place in effecting this downgrade movement of society. These are—first, the distaste for a simple and laborious life...

Pope Leo XIII goes on to explain how this manifests itself:

> In the workman, it evinces itself in a tendency to desert his trade, to shrink from toil, to become discontented with his lot, to fix his gaze on things that are above him, and to look forward with unthinking hopefulness to some future equalization of property...
>
> Men's minds become a prey to jealousy and heart-burnings, rights are openly trampled underfoot, and, finally, the people, betrayed in their expectations, attack public order, and place themselves in conflict with those who are charged to maintain it.

I suppose if I name specific examples of movements provoking such things I will wind up getting into blog wars with their various defenders. Needless to say, there is no shortage of all of that going on today (civil disobedience, betrayed expectations, and lawlessness). Often the anger does not only come from the lowest classes, but from the most privileged.

Pope Leo XIII had a remedy for these evils. The remedy will not be satisfactory to those intellectuals who are not satisfied with anything unless it is comprehensive, nor will it be for those activists who mask their desire for vengeance with demands of justice in their moral vanity. The remedy is meditation on the joyful mysteries of the Holy Rosary.

Here the pontiff explains what we will find when meditating on those early years of the life of Christ:

Here is the patient industry which provides what is
required for food and raiment; which does so "in the
sweat of the brow," which is contented with little,
and which seeks rather to diminish the number of
its wants than to multiply the sources of its wealth.

In this teaching we find the spirit of St. Peter. The Catholic Church in its institution or its members does not have
enough "gold and silver" to end poverty, but what we have is
Jesus and that is what (or rather, Who) we can give people.
With Jesus, poverty can go from unbearable to sweet: just
look at the lives of the Saints. If we do not teach that possessions often hinder rather than help in the quest for salvation, then people will conclude that poverty is something to
be striven against, rather than striven for.

If we tell the man with a dollar that his suffering is in
vain and that he need not be patient in it then surely he will
not be. If we tell the rich man that poverty is to be avoided
he will probably make sure he has more than enough for
himself, and not be generous in almsgiving. Both lead to
more consequences here and in eternity.

"The power of God takes away or gives with the same
ease in matters temporal as in matters spiritual," said the
Little Flower in an apparition as she provided money to a
community of nuns in desperate need.[1] If we preach prayer
in the name of Jesus Christ, men can ask God for their
needs, and He will grant them! The poor can have hope
rather than burn with envy, and the rich will not worry
about suffering want from being overly generous.

If we preach the Holy Rosary to all and teach its mysteries so mankind can meditate on the humble life of labor and
poverty of our Lord, then the poor man strives to endure
like Christ, and the rich man seeks to give alms generously

---

[1]   See Elizabeth Ficocelli, *Shower of Heavenly Roses: Stories of
the Intercession of St. Therese of Lisieux* (Chestnut Ridge, PA:
Crossroad, 2004).

in order to become more like Christ. I for one will not be putting any confidence in our Pope, President, Congress, or leaders to end poverty or provide for our needs. Rather let us all put our hope in our Heavenly King and Queen and ask for our needs while meditating and saying the Holy Rosary.

Queen of the Holy Rosary, Pray for Us!

18

Joshua the Contemplative

🍀

There is much talk these days about "going out to the peripheries" and of finding a "use" for contemplative religious orders whose charisms have not traditionally been activist. The modern world has a very difficult time understanding the contemplative tradition. As far back as the late Enlightenment, the heretic Emperor Joseph II of Austria lent his name to the heresy of *Josephism* which taught that only the active orders could be considered "useful;" a century later Pope Leo XIII censured the heresy of Americanism, which among other things, prioritized the active over the passive virtues, thus inverting the traditional hierarchy of values.

Yes, there is the momentum building for everybody in the Catholic religious world, even contemplatives, to "get out there" and "do" something. The contemplative tradition is increasingly viewed as something self-absorbed, something that turns one inward and makes one oblivious to the suffering around us.

This is a tragic underestimation of the value of contemplative life. Persons promoting this idea fail to realize that the active and contemplative go together; the contemplative tradition is what creates the dynamic strength that makes the active fruitful. To denigrate the contemplative or seek to reduce it at the expense of the active is also to destroy the active works of the Church. Incidentally, this is why so many programs and active efforts of the Church in the modern world fail. The contemplative serves as the basis of strength for the active. When the contemplative is cut off, the active withers like a branch deprived of water.

We could refute this attack on contemplative life by reference to the lives of the saints, which provide us with ample evidence to the contrary. But to keep this brief, let us appeal rather to the Sacred Scriptures, where the person of Joshua furnishes us with a marvelous example of the contemplative who bears rich fruit.

Joshua as a contemplative? The warrior? Yes, you have read correctly. Joshua is of course known for leading the children of Israel in the conquest of the Holy Land, presiding over her armies as a sort of military ruler. But what is less known is that Joshua had an extraordinarily intense spiritual life and spent years and silent contemplation before the Lord, before God elevated him to lead the hosts of Israel.

Let us turn to the Book of Exodus, where we read of how God used to address Moses in the Tent of Meeting, where the Ark of the Covenant was housed, that holiest relic of Israel that represented the tangible presence of God among His people:

> Now Moses used to take the tent and pitch it outside the camp, far off from the camp; he called it the tent of meeting. And everyone who sought the Lord would go out to the tent of meeting, which was outside the camp. Whenever Moses went out to the tent, all the people would rise and stand, each of them, at the entrance of their tents and watch Moses until he had gone into the tent. When Moses entered the tent, the pillar of cloud would descend and stand at the entrance of the tent, and the Lord would speak with Moses. When all the people saw

the pillar of cloud standing at the entrance of the tent, all the people would rise and bow down, all of them, at the entrance of their tents. Thus the Lord used to speak to Moses face to face, as one speaks to a friend. Then he would return to the camp; *but his young assistant, Joshua son of Nun, would not leave the tent.* (Exod. 33:7–11)

Here we see the spiritual formation of Joshua before he succeeded Moses. Joshua spends his days inside the Tabernacle, alone with God. What must this have been like! Hour after hour prostrate before the visible presence of God, which was manifest by the pillar of the cloud whenever Moses approached. When I sit alone in Eucharistic Adoration, I often imagine myself in the place of Joshua, sitting alone in front of the Ark of the Covenant and the awesome mystery it represented.

How long did Joshua spend before the Presence of God? We do not know; this particular episode narrated above happened immediately after the Exodus, but since this arrangement continued throughout the forty years in the wilderness, we may reasonably surmise that this was the practice of Joshua throughout the entirety of those forty years. This means that before Joshua ever led a single battle in the Holy Land or waged any of his famous campaigns, he spent upwards of *forty years* in regular—perhaps daily— adoration of God silently inside the Tabernacle.

We also read that Joshua was present with Moses on Mount Sinai when the Law was received. We all know the story of Moses receiving the Law, but we seldom recall that others were present on the mount as well. Exodus 24:9–11 states that beside Moses, Aaron and his sons, as well as seventy elders went up on the mountain and beheld the face of God, feasting in the divine presence. Joshua is not mentioned here, but later in episode of the golden calf, it is revealed that Joshua was on the mountain with Moses when the Law was received, for he accompanied Moses down from Sinai and was the first to hear the sound of revelry in the camp, which he initially mistook for a battle from a distance (cf. Exod. 32:17–18).

How long was Joshua on Sinai? We do not know, but he appears to have been acting in the position of Moses' personal assistant. If so, there is no reason to suppose he was not on the mountain the entire forty days, probably standing a far off to maintain his distance from the frightful theophanies being experienced by Moses. And what was he doing for that time? We may reasonably suppose the same thing he does in the succeeding years sitting in the Tabernacle: adoring the presence of God.

All in all, the picture we get of Joshua in the Book of Exodus is of a man who passionately desired the Presence of God. Yes, he went on to do mighty works; in his warfare and the worldly, administrative concerns that will envelop him after Moses' death he is undoubtedly a Martha. But prior to assuming this role, we see him spending decades of formation in what can best be described as a contemplative tradition—countless hours in the silent adoration of the mystery of God's presence. In his formation and the desires of his heart, he is a Mary.

In the Book of Joshua, Joshua is one who discerns the voice of God and is able to carry out His will. Are we to think that those long years silently adoring the Presence of God did not have something to do with this? Indeed, we see in Joshua that the source of his fruitfulness in his worldly endeavors was probably tied directly to his sensitivity to the Spirit of God, as formed through countless years in God's presence.

Contemplative spirituality and contemplative religious orders are not "useless," and it is a tremendous error to view their value only in terms of how much they can "open up" to "doing something" evangelical. The contemplative life has always been valued higher than the active life, both in the absolute sense, and in the sense that even the fruitful exercise of an active ministry presupposes a strong grounding in the interior life.

The Israelites were prone to grumbling. We may imagine contemporaries in Joshua's own day accusing him of being self-absorbed for spending so many hours in silent adoration before God; he no doubt may have come off as "closed," maybe "sad" and even "funereal" at times for the gravity of the mystery he was adoring. Perhaps at times aloof, seeming "anesthetized" to the goings on of the world around him. Had we known Joshua in person, like many other saintly men and women, we may have found him to be a "real downer." Some may have urged him to stop being so "enclosed" and to get himself out "to the peripheries." But ultimately, had Joshua not spent those precious years in formation—and a very intensive formation the likes of which we can hardly imagine—it is doubtful whether he would have been the successful leader he became.

The power to shout and knock down walls flows from humble worship in the Presence of the Holy One. If we wish to do the former, we cannot neglect the latter.

19

Alcuin to Higbald: A Christian View on Temporal Misfortune

❧

To what degree is it appropriate to view temporal calamities as a chastisement from God? A mass shooting, an abuse scandal, a tragic death from disease, a national tragedy. We have all grappled with these sorts of events. We know that all things that happen are permitted by God for some purpose in His grand providence. But saying such seems to be coolly received these days, if not downright callous, as people have a difficult time attributing any non-positive act in the world to God's agency—even though we know from revelation that God destroys cities, sends plagues, marks people for destruction, and once flooded the entirety of human civilization.

What, then, is an appropriate way to view these sorts of tragedies? How can we come to terms with them in a way that builds our faith rather than turns us into bitter skeptics?

Let us begin by going back to a letter from the Anglo-Saxon scholar Alcuin to the monk Higbald, penned around 793. At the time Alcuin was heading up Charlemagne's educational reforms from Aachen in France, while his old friend Higbald was abbot of the renowned monastery of Lindisfarne in Northumbria, England. Lindisfarne had just suffered a devastating attack from the Vikings. Many monks had been killed or enslaved, and the monastery church was pillaged and desecrated. News of the raid shocked the Christian world. When Alcuin heard about it, he wrote his old friend a letter to console him in his sorrow.

The letter is interesting because Alcuin's method of consolation is to remind Higbald that calamities are a gesture of God's love. Let us consider the letter at length, because it provides an interesting window into the minds of these 8th century monks and how they processed the reality of evil:

> You who survive, stand like men, fight bravely and defend the camp of God. Remember how Judas Maccabaeus cleansed the Temple and freed the people from a foreign yoke. If anything needs correction in your way of gentleness, correct it quickly...
> Do not glory in the vanity of dress; that is cause for shame, not boasting, in priests and servants of God. Do not blur the words of your prayers by drunkenness. Do not go out after the indulgences of the flesh and the greed of the world, but stand firm in the service of God and the discipline of the monastic life, that the holy fathers whose sons you are may not cease to protect you. May you remain safe through their prayers, as you walk in their footsteps. Do not be degenerate sons, having such fathers. They will not cease protecting you, if they see you following their example.
> Do not be dismayed by this disaster. God chastises every son whom he accepts, so perhaps he has chastised you more because he loves you more. Jerusalem, a city loved by God was destroyed, with the Temple of God, in Babylonian flames. Rome, surrounded by its company of holy apostles and countless martyrs, was devastated by the heathen, but quickly recovered through the goodness of God.

Almost the whole of Europe had been denuded with fire and sword by Goths and Huns, but now by God's mercy is as bright with churches as the sky with stars and in them the offices of the Christian religion grow and flourish. Encourage each other, saying, "Let us return to the Lord our God, for he is very forgiving and never deserts those who hope in him."

And you, holy father, leader of God's people, shepherd of a holy flock, physician of souls, light set on a candlestick, be a model of all goodness to all who can see you, a herald of salvation to all who hear you. May your community be of exemplary character, to bring others to life, not to damnation. Let your dinners be sober, not drunken. Let your clothes befit your station. Do not copy the men of the world in vanity, for vain dress and useless adornment are a reproach to you before men and a sin before God. It is better to dress your immortal soul in good ways than to deck with fine clothes the body that soon rots in dust. Clothe and feed Christ in the poor, that so doing you may reign with Christ. Redemption is a man's true riches. If we loved gold we should send it to heaven to be kept there for us. We have what we love: let us love the eternal which will not perish.

When our lord King Charles returns from defeating his enemies, by God's mercy, I plan to go to him, and if I can then do anything for you about the boys who have been carried off by the pagans as prisoners or about any other of your needs, I shall make every effort to see that it is done. Fare well, beloved in Christ, and be ever strengthened in well-doing.

It is fascinating that Alcuin thought the appropriate response to the tragedy was to remind Higbald of things that offend God, as well as to point out that the horrific murder of the Lindisfarne monks should be construed as an act of love, as "God chastises every son whom he accepts, so perhaps he has chastised you more because he loves you more."

Alcuin is here offering a classical explanation for evil that comes from St. Augustine: temporal misfortunes fall equally on the good and evil; the difference is not in what befalls, but in how people respond to it. The purposes for suffering amongst persons are distinct, despite the external similarity in the nature of the ills. In *City of God*, St. Augustine says:

> There is, too, a very great difference in the purpose served both by those events which we call adverse and those called prosperous. For the good man is neither uplifted with the good things of time, nor broken by its ills; but the wicked man, because he is corrupted by this world's happiness, feels himself punished by its unhappiness.
>
> Yet often, even in the present distribution of temporal things, does God plainly evince His own interference. For if every sin were now visited with manifest punishment, nothing would seem to be reserved for the final judgment; on the other hand, if no sin received now a plainly divine punishment, it would be concluded that there is no divine providence at all. And so of the good things of this life: if God did not by a very visible liberality confer these on some of those persons who ask for them, we should say that these good things were not at His disposal; and if He gave them to all who sought them, we should suppose that such were the only rewards of His service; and such a service would make us not godly, but greedy rather, and covetous.

Wherefore, though good and bad men suffer alike, we must not suppose that there is no difference between the men themselves, because there is no difference in what they both suffer. For even in the likeness of the sufferings, there remains an unlikeness in the sufferers; and though exposed to the same anguish, virtue and vice are not the same thing. For as the same fire causes gold to glow brightly, and chaff to smoke; and under the same flail the straw is beaten small, while the grain is cleansed; and as the lees are not mixed with the oil, though squeezed out of the vat by the same pressure, so the same violence of affliction proves, purges, clarifies the good, but damns, ruins, exterminates the wicked. And thus it is that in the same affliction the wicked detest God and blaspheme, while the good pray and praise. So material a difference does it make, not what ills are suffered, but what kind of man suffers them. For, stirred up with the same movement, mud exhales a horrible stench, and ointment emits a fragrant odor (Book 1.8).

Of course, pointing this out is generally not welcome advice when a friend is suffering. A person who just lost a child to leukemia does not want to be told they should use the occasion as an opportunity to grow in holiness. They want empathy more than anything else. And to be fair, Higbald and Alcuin were monks whose charism was to learn to see God in every aspect of life, so they operated under elevated standards. But so, too, must we lay people, in our own way, attempt to see God in our trials. While we must always extend empathy and compassion to those who are suffering ("weep with those who weep," [Rom. 12:15]), in our own hearts we should bear in mind that God's love for us does

not preclude us from suffering terrible calamities, personally or corporately.

The real take-away is this: when something bad happens,
the question we should be asking is not "Was this a punishment from God?" The answer to that will differ for every
single person. But if we are in Christ, we must affirm that
"all things work together for good to them that love God"
(Rom. 8:28). Is that something we really believe? Have we
really internalized that maxim? Or is it just something we
repeat because we don't know what else to say in the face of
calamity? Regardless of where we are in our spiritual lives,
our peace will be much greater to the degree I can really cry
Romans 8:28 from the depths of my heart.

20

Waves of Darkness

✤

Not long ago I published a piece called "Alcuin to Higbald on the Christian View of Temporal Disasters." This essay concerned an interesting letter I came across from the Carolingian era monk Alcuin writing to Abbot Higbald of Lindisfarne. Alcuin sought to console his friend Higbald after his monastery was sacked by Vikings. Alcuin essentially told Higbald, "This, too, is an act of God's love. Use it as an occasion to better yourself, pray more, and move on." I highlighted this as an example of the traditional way Christians contextualized disasters within their lives.

After publication, a reader contacted me with the following comments, which I will quote in their entirety:

> I find explanations like this sufficient for car crashes and cancers...but we are dealing with something more which tempts me to doubt. We have all heard that God, when He is truly angry with his people, will send them wolves rather than pastors. Here in the United States, at least, the people have always voted down issues like abortion and gay marriage, when given the chance. These crimes are thrust upon us by the courts and duplicitous politicians. It is so bad today, that every single institution in the world, is run by evil people who hate God, and hate

the people under their charge. So it is not enough that we have a fallen nature and tend towards sin. It is not enough that we are tempted constantly by evil angelic powers who are super-intelligent and have access to our imaginations and never sleep. It is not enough that we are surrounded by the general misbehavior of our fellow humans and the weakness of the flesh, and all the things that make the World a dangerous place for our souls.

No, it is not enough.

In these times, we also have every single institution, worldwide, run by human devils that actively seek to corrupt us, destroy our families, and enslave us. It is these human devils that control politics, media, war, economics, education, art, music, commerce, entertainment, leisure, science, healthcare, law, infrastructure, and so on. And these human devils have all the money, all the power, and all the voice, far above any simple sheep.

On top of all that, the Catholic Religion is almost completely shattered. The hierarchy is cowardly at best, shameful most often, and heretical at worst. There are no two priests that preach the same thing. A close look at the Novus Ordo, the Traditional Latin Mass, and the Byzantine rites appear to be almost completely different religions. (Although, at the moment, the Sacraments seem to be relatively preserved, thank God.) Constant scandal makes evangelization very difficult, if not impossible. And us sheep—to whom most of these questions are way above our paygrade—are forced to walk the line between deciding what is true, on the one hand, and on the other, risk becoming protestant/our own pope.

Yet God wills all men to be saved. And the saints assure us that most souls will perish into an eternal hell. I don't know why we all don't collapse in despair. We have no saints, no signs, and no signal graces. Just a book that purports to be God's Word, though we are often told by the "experts" it is no such thing. We have an institution that purports to be Divine, but its leaders and teachers display tendencies that are more diabolic. And we have a world that has, for the most part, forced God out of their daily lives, more through ignorance than choice.

How are we supposed to save our own souls, let alone help save those of our children, our loved ones, our neighbors, and others? Or do we just wait for God to smite us, write off all the sinners of whatever category, and hope to rebuild if we live through whatever is coming? Thoughts like these terrify me.

This is a doozy of a comment. He brings up a lot of things. Constant scandals. Liturgical chaos. "Human devils" that control all aspects of life. He mentions politics, media, war, economics, education, art, music, commerce, entertainment, leisure, science, healthcare, law, infrastructure, and so on. Money and power in the hands of the enemy. Every institution under the sway of darkness. Unrelenting war against the family. Cowardly hierarchy. A veritable litany of chaos.

When I read this comment, my response is, "Friend, who told you to worry about such things?" When were these problems entrusted to your care? What does our Lord say? "Therefore, do not worry about tomorrow, for tomorrow will worry about itself. Each day has enough trouble of its own" (Matt. 6:34). I am convinced that this passage from the Beatitudes is instrumental in staving off despair. The commenter is right—power, influence, money, media, institutions—all of it is under the power of the evil one. Little has changed since the beginning: "And the devil said unto him, 'All this power will I give thee, and the glory of them: for that is delivered unto me; and to whomsoever I will I give it.'" (Luke 4:5-7). But none of that is my business. My response to this evil is the same as Christ's: "Worship the Lord thy God, and Him alone shall you serve." None of those other issues are my problem.

Our Lord told us to focus on today, on what is before us, on our small little sphere of influence that God has entrusted to us: "Aspire to live quietly, to mind your own affairs" (1 Thess. 4:11), "that we may lead quiet and peaceable lives" (1 Tim. 2:2). I don't have the resources to fix all or even any of the world's problems. Christ asks us to only be faithful with the little we have been entrusted with. To those who have been given much, much will be required. Those with ten talents will have to account for how they invested those ten talents. But, my friends, the vast majority of us can have no influence on these matters. And since we cannot, what good does it do to worry about them? What does the Psalmist say?

> O Lord, my heart is not lifted up,
> my eyes are not raised too high;
> I do not occupy myself with things
> too great and too marvelous for me (Ps. 131:1)

I cannot speak for anyone else, but my faith has been strengthened by the events of the last few years. Or rather, not by those events, but how God has helped me find peace despite them. I feel like I have finally made real strides in my spiritual life, overcoming things I struggled with for years. God's providence has never seemed so real, and it becomes ever easier to see the working of grace in my day-to-day life. I have a deeper peace and more profound sense of God's mercy than I have in years past. That's just my experience. I understand that for someone who is in crisis, that will certainly not be their experience. But don't tell me my religion is "broken" because *you* are in crisis. *My faith* is not in crisis, and nothing is broken *for me*.

One might say that such a solipsistic approach is merely sticking my head in the sand, ignoring the very real problems in the world that are destroying souls and making a shipwreck of faith. I disagree. I know these problems are real, and I do what I can to combat them within the sphere of my influence. But that little sphere is all I have responsibility over; beyond that, I commend it all to God. Maybe I am excessively focused on my own affairs. But the reality is, that's all I am responsible for. Why load yourself up with the responsibilities to save the world, Church, and civilization? Are the crosses Jesus has given you not heavy enough? Are your sins so miniscule that you need to worry about the sins of everyone else?

The great paradox is this: Focusing on the little things God entrusts to us is not turning our back on the world and the Church. It is, in fact, the only way to save them. Christendom was not created because a lot of angry men got together to criticize the government and the hierarchy or create a "movement" to address it. It was created because a man went out in the desert to be alone with God; because a man walked on the beach with his friend and had a heart to heart conversation about Christ, because a woman decided she wanted to dedicate her virginity to God; because a Roman rhetorician went out into a garden to weep for his sins; because a man decided to live in a cave on the slopes of Mount Subiaco; because a slave boy prayed a hundred times a night alone before a roughhewn wooden cross jabbed into the rocky slopes of Mount Slemish[1] while he watched sheep; because a solitary Jesuit father, isolated and suffer-

---

[1] The hillside in County Antrim, Ireland, where St. Patrick tended sheep as a slave. See St. Patrick's *Confessions*, Chap. 16

ing immensely from his captors' torments, carved crosses in the trunks of trees in the wilderness of New York; because a priest decided to work and die with some lepers on the other side of the world. Because the Son of God—when faced with all the hatred and sin and darkness the world had to offer—chose to be silent and do nothing. In such acts was Christendom formed, and in such acts shall our Faith be preserved.

Be faithful to whatever little is entrusted to you in your own sphere of influence. You own little life is all you must focus on. Stay grounded there and you will have a much better chance of weathering the waves of darkness rushing over the world. You will stand on the rock while the towers of sand fall about you.

21

The Law of the Harvest[†]

❧

*For they sow the wind, and they shall reap the whirl-
wind (Hos. 8:7).*

In the book of the Old Testament prophet Hosea, God
warns the Israelites of the consequences of protracted
disobedience against His commandments. "They sow the
wind," God says, "and they shall reap the whirlwind." In the
same passage, the Lord makes another agricultural analogy,
asking them to consider the impossibility of making meal
from a headless stalk of grain: "The standing grain has no
heads, it shall yield no meal."

Scripture often uses the images of sowing and reaping
to explain spiritual truths. It is, in fact, one of the most
common metaphors in the Bible. Let us meditate on just
a few of the better-known passages pertaining to sowing
and reaping:

+ "And Isaac sowed in that land and reaped in the same
  year a hundredfold. The Lord blessed him" (Gen. 26:12).
+ "Those who plow iniquity and sow trouble reap the
  same" (Job 4:8).
+ "Those who sow in tears shall reap with shouts of joy!
  He who goes out weeping, bearing the seed for sowing,

[†] Previously unpublished essay.

shall come home with shouts of joy, bringing his sheaves with him" (Ps. 126:5–6).

+ "One who sows righteousness gets a sure reward" (Prov. 11:18).
+ "Whoever sows injustice will reap calamity" (Prov. 22:8).
+ "He who sows sparingly will also reap sparingly, and he who sows bountifully will also reap bountifully" (2 Cor. 9:6).
+ "Whatsoever a man sows, that also shall he reap" (Gal. 6:7).

A more exhaustive study would undoubtedly yield even more examples. The metaphor is used with such frequency that we may presume a general spiritual principle that runs through all these verses, a golden thread binding them all together and constituting a rule of Christian life—call it a "Law of the Harvest." The Law of the Harvest is comprised of three general principles:

The first is that *you reap what you sow*. Things reproduce according to their kind. In agriculture, if you sow corn seeds, you reap corn; if you plant peas, you will harvest peas. This is common sense, but we tend to forget the principle when applied to the spiritual life. Whatever you sow, you will reap according to its kind. If you sow skepticism, you will reap doubt. If you sow hatred, you will reap broken relationships. If you sow sloth, you will reap goals unaccomplished. If you sow sin, you will reap death.

But fortunately, the same holds true for things good and true: Sow friendship, reap love. Sow contentment, reap peacefulness. Sow prayer, reap sanctity. We must leave off thinking that our life is a series of unconnected coincidences, external impositions that merely "happen" to us as passive objects. In most cases, the way our life unfolds is determined by the choices we make. What we reap is determined by what we sow. Therefore let us sow the same kinds of things we hope to reap.

The second principle of the Law of the Harvest is *you reap after you sow*. To return to our agricultural analogy, a farmer knows that after he plants, he must let time go by before it is time to sow. "For everything there is a season, and a time for every matter under heaven...a time to plant, and a time to pluck up what is planted" (Eccl. 3:1–2). He would be a foolish farmer who sowed his seed and expected to find a fully matured crop the following morning. Such is the stuff of fairy tales, but not of serious agriculture.

Similarly, we must accept that the spiritual life is a game of endurance. This is why St. Paul so frequently compares it to a race (cf. 1 Cor. 9:24; Heb. 12:1; 2 Tim. 4:7). We must think of the spiritual life like exercise. It is no coincidence that the root of the words "ascetic" or an "asceticism" is *ascesis*, the Greek word commonly rendered as "training." Progress in the spiritual life consists in training ourselves in the discipline of God—and this takes time. No one goes to the gym and expects to see gains on their first day; they understand that results are found in consistent activity over the long term.

While God certainly can give us graces to grow quickly, more often than not He allows us to struggle with our sins as a way of building our strength. If I am spotting my friend while he is bench pressing, I may occasionally use my hands to support the bar, but what benefit would it be if I did this every time? To make gains in strength training, one must bear the brunt of the weights. Recall how in the Old Testament, God did not drive all the Canaanites from the Promised Land at once; rather, He permitted them to remain, that the Israelites might wrestle with them and come to rely on God's providence. The spiritual life is no different; we must be prepared for a long struggle, for victories which will come in time as we are slowly transformed under the gentle workings of grace.

The final principle is that *you reap more than you sow.* Think of the size of seed of wheat compared to the mature wheat stalk, or a six foot high corn stalk compared to the size of a tiny corn seed. Or, to use a human analogy, the size of a full-grown adult in the splendor of his manhood compared to the size of the microscopic sperm that planted him in his mother's womb. What is reaped is vastly larger than what is sown.

If only we understood the spiritual application of this principle! Our spiritual lives are like a kind of investment. Most of us understand the power of compound interest; if you were to invest only a single penny with the guarantee that your investment would double every day, at the end of thirty days you would have around $5.3 million dollars. The investment we make in our spiritual lives is similar—it compounds, either under the power of grace if we do our works in Christ, or under the corruption of evil if we give ourselves over to sin. This is true in two senses:

First, as it relates to the formation of habits. He who indulgences in sin becomes habituated to sin. His conscience becomes dulled, and sin comes easier to him than before. He gives himself over to worse vices. What began as a drip becomes a torrent. The little sins he sowed have led to entire habits of sin that dominate his entire person. And the same is true with habits of virtue.

Second, as it relates to rewards and punishments in the next life. He who sows in virtue will be rewarded by God; if he has been a faithful investor with God's talents, he will be told "enter into your master's happiness" (Matt. 25:23). Similarly, he who scorns the life of virtue will reap weeping and gnashing of teeth reserved for those cast into the outer darkness.

Understanding the Law of the Harvest can help us to

approach the spiritual life in a rational manner, with proper expectations and the correct work ethic. Just as a farmer must understand the principles of agricultural planting to reap a rich harvest, so must we be cognizant of these spiritual principles if we wish to "reap with shouts of joy" (Ps. 126:5).

22

Leniency and Severity

❧

Have you ever reflected on how your judgment of whether you are harsh or lenient with a particular sin is colored by your own experience?

We tend to assume that everyone starts on a level playing field—that when it comes to virtue and vice, we are all a blank slate, and our experience of temptation and sin is uniform. Perhaps this is true in the sense that nobody is born having committed any actual sin, nor with any particular virtue. But we must not forget that we all have certain natural dispositions inherent in our personality. These dispositions not only make us disposed to certain kinds of vices and virtues, but also affect our culpability or merit respectively.

For example, a certain person by nature has an extremely gregarious personality: extroverted, talkative, sociable. Because of his gregarious nature, he is susceptible to the sin of gossip and falls easily into it. But another man by nature is reserved and solemn, not given to much talk in general, let alone the sin of gossip in particular. The former can scarcely go a few days without gossiping, while the latter has probably never committed the sin in his life.

The silent, reserved man might look at the chatterbox and feel irritated and judgmental about the latter's proclivity to gossip. From his perspective, it is not a difficult thing

115

to refrain from gossip and he is annoyed that the other cannot exercise the restraint that he himself exhibits. *He* has no problems refraining from gossip. Why can't the other refrain with similar ease?

What this man does not realize is that it is not his great virtue that restrains him from gossiping—he merely has a personality that is not disposed to it. Because he is not disposed to it, there is no struggle for him in refraining from this sin. Because he experiences no struggle, he can't understand that other people do. Because he can't understand this, he can't empathize. Because he can't empathize, he judges the other for his sin. And his assessment of his own virtue is distorted.

But what of his own sin? He may not be disposed to gossip, but he is certainly disposed to other sins. Perhaps because he is withdrawn he is often lonely, and turns to pornography now and then in vain hopes of consoling his loneliness. This is a struggle he understands. He is deeply embarrassed by it. He fully experiences the temptation and the difficulty surrounding this sin. Because it's hard, he wants empathy—and he easily gives empathy to others struggling with pornography as well. He is much less likely to judge himself or others for this sin. He is much more likely to feel like, "Nobody's perfect. I know I've got my faults, but I'm trying." He is more lenient with himself and others because he feels this struggle more keenly.

We are most critical of those sins we are not naturally disposed to commit anyway, while we are most lenient towards those sins we ourselves struggle with. Our own experience tends to be the lens through which we apportion severity or leniency to a particular sin. We think we are being fair, we think we are being level-headed—but really we are simply justifying ourselves.

Of course, certain sins are objectively worse than others. Murder is worse than cheating on an exam, and I would argue pornography is worse than gossiping. But how much virtue we exercise in overcoming a particular sin is very relative to our own strengths and weaknesses. A man who struggles with a porn habit and, through prayer and much effort, manages to go three weeks without relapse may have exercised more virtue in this regard than a man who is not easily disposed to temptations of the flesh and has never looked at porn in his life. The man who, through grace-filled effort, manages to restrain himself from gossiping throughout Lent has exercised more fortitude than the man who isn't disposed to gossip to begin with.

This is because virtue is not merely doing the right thing—it is doing the right thing *habitually*, because you have disciplined yourself to do so. A person who has learned to be unperturbed through discipline has acquired the virtue of patience. A person who is naturally unperturbed by things has considerably less patience, at least considered as a virtue.

Through the gift of wisdom, may we see with God's eyes and truly focus on removing the plank from our own eye.

23

Escaping Our Subjectivity

❧

These days are very challenging times for people. Sadly, I think I witnessed more religious acquaintances lose faith or at least suffer grave doubts recently than ever before. Undergoing a crisis of faith is a terribly jarring experience and I pray for the peace of anyone who has suffered through it.

Considering this, is there anything we can say about the patterns that emerge when people undergo a crisis of faith, especially as it plays out in the interactions with others whose faith is intact on social media? Then we shall consider, as people of faith, how to best engage with those who are struggling.

When someone talks about their crisis of faith online, the back-and-forth that ensues in the comment thread is always of great interest to me. In these exchanges I have noticed that the conversation between the person whose faith is suffering and the person whose faith is intact seems to break down. Neither one seems capable or interested in hearing the other. And neither side seems aware of it.

First, the persons whose faith remains intact often seem to over-rationalize the experience of the doubter. Faith, even if it is grounded intellectual affirmation, is not *merely* an intellectual act. It is a kind of assent, a "giving of ourselves" over to a proposition. It involves our will and passion. It is not only believing the truth but orienting one's life towards it and—by extension—loving that towards which we orient ourselves. The theological virtues are integrated, not isolated. Josef Pieper wrote in his treatise *Faith, Hope, Love* that the theological virtues are acquired in one order but lost in reverse order. We begin with faith; faith engenders hope; and hope gives birth to love. But the process is reversed in the case of one who loses faith: first, their love towards the object of their faith (God or the Church) grows cold. The coldness of love causes hope to wither. With hope and love dried up, there is nothing left to nourish faith, which is extinguished last of all.

This means that the process by which we came to faith from unbelief is not the same process that is needed when confronting doubt in one who already believes (or used to believe); or, to put it simply, the way in and the way *back* in are not through the same door. Reading Chesterton might bring you to the faith, but it is less likely to save the faith of one who is wavering. A person who begins to doubt the Church is not unaware of the arguments in the Church's favor. Indeed, this person may very well have been converted in the past through the very same arguments. Their issue is not that they don't grasp the reasoning, but that the Church, as an object of affection, is no longer desirable. This means the act of doubt is taking place outside of the realm of pure reason.

If you nod haughtily and say, "Yeah that's right, people who doubt are being irrational," stop yourself right there. It is true that this act of doubt does not take place in the realm of reason, but that does not make it any less comprehensible. A problem is no less real or valid just because it might not be rational. In education we have a dictum that, "They don't care what you know until they know that you care." This means you cannot expect a student to learn if they do not believe you have their best interest in mind. I cannot habitually belittle, denigrate, and humiliate a student and expect him to master the algebra I am teaching him. He will have a visceral reaction against *me* and everything associated with me. Part of him will intentionally *not* want to learn just to spite me. He will feel helpless against me; the one, solitary way that remains for him to exercise autonomy is simply to close his mind off to whatever I tell him. It doesn't matter how logical the algebraic formulations are; he simply does not want what I am offering. By contrast, a student who feels affirmed and encouraged by their teacher yields their mind readily to instruction and the educational dynamic becomes fruitful and even pleasant.

Dr. Peter Kwasniewski made a similar point in a recent article in *Crisis* called, "In the Midst of Crisis, Be Driven by Faith, Not Fear." One of the many take aways of this excellent reflection is that people who lose faith often have focused too much on the Church's human element. This may be the case. They have accustomed themselves to focusing only on the failures of flesh-and-blood slobs who manage the institutional aspect of things. This is only part of the picture, however, for it needs to be understood that when a person has suffered extensively at the hands of that "human element," faith is no longer an issue of merely understanding the arguments or "taking the long view." The doubter has a visceral, guttural reaction against the Church that cannot be addressed by appeals to reason. A person who suffered war trauma from combat may duck when they hear any loud popping noise, and it is useless to try to reason with them that the war is over and there is nothing to fear.

This is why Catholics who have lost faith are no longer swayed by "the arguments." They are familiar with them, but the arguments "no longer satisfy," or they "just don't cut it" anymore. They don't work because the person's crisis is not primarily intellectual; it is rather that they no longer experience Catholicism as something desirable. An argument in service of a truth that is undesirable will not produce assent. You may present me with rock-solid arguments grounded in reason and empirical data that the United States is going to eventually become subservient to China. But if that truth is not desirable to me, the strength of your argument will do nothing to make me embrace it. I may indeed fight against it even though I recognize the strength of the argument.

So this is the first thing I would say: those whose faith is intact need to understand that one who doubts often does so outside the realm of pure reason. Persons whose faith is intact are accomplishing nothing by trying to present doubting Catholics with "the arguments." Let go of your rationalism. Do not treat this as if it is solely a problem with the doubter's intellect.

Now, on the other hand, the person who doubts tends to think wrongly that their own doubt constitutes an existential problem for the Catholic religion *in general.* Their anecdotal experiences become the standard of truth. Because the arguments "just don't satisfy" them, they mistakenly think the arguments lack validity. Sometimes they are immune to the force of argument from over-exposure. The truth that once dazzled them and expanded their intellect is now a rote platitude devoid of power. They think this is because the maxim is not compelling, not because they have become numb to it.

People have a regrettable tendency to universalize their own experiences. This means that if *they* have a problem, then there *is* a problem. They have an issue or hang up with something, and suddenly the entire edifice is compromised—"crippled," "broken," or whatever adjective they choose. They have a hard time imagining that their experience is not indicative of a more universal truth; and this only gets reinforced as others pour out of the woodwork with their own anecdotal stories that agree. The problem is not with them, it is with the "broken" institution or system of belief as a whole, whose brokenness seems so self-evident that those who do not see it appear as naïve. They think their crisis is due entirely to problems inherent to the Church or its philosophy.

This whole issue is really one of perspective. It is extremely difficult to escape the parameters of our own subjectivity. But this cuts both ways as well: People who do not have a problem can errantly assume there is no problem just because they don't have one. They easily reconcile disparate poles that others cannot. Their peace is not disturbed, and so they have a hard time empathizing with those whose peace has been shattered. They often assume the person who is wavering in faith is "not being logical about it."

Both suffer from an inability to escape their own subjectivity. Just because you have a problem does not mean the Church has a problem. And just because you have no problem does not mean no problem exists. Ultimately, the problem is not just with the doubter, nor just with the Church. The crux of the problem exists on a subjective plane, at the crossroads where the Church and the doubter intersect in an *experience* that precipitates the crisis of faith.

Both doubter and the faithful have a difficult time understanding this: the doubter does not want it to be *his* problem; he wants it to be a problem with the Church— that way his doubt is justified, and he can be at peace with his conscience. The person of intact faith does not want to confront the doubter's experience; he would rather reduce the matter to a series of dry intellectual propositions that the doubter needs to affirm. He does this because he does not want to consider that the arguments that are sufficient for *him* are not sufficient for someone else.

And thus we all talk past each other because we cannot get away from making our subjective experiences the ground of our approach.

24

The Perfecting of Every Work and the Holy Car Ride[†]

※

In the *Imitation of Christ* we read the following tale:

A certain man, being in anxiety of mind, continually tossed about between hope and fear, and being on a certain day overwhelmed with grief, cast himself down in prayer before the altar in a church, and meditated within himself, saying, "Oh! if I but knew that I should still persevere," and presently heard within him a voice from God, "And if thou didst know it, what wouldst thou do? Do now what thou wouldst do then, and thou shalt be very secure." And straightway being comforted and strengthened, he committed himself to the will of God and the perturbation of spirit ceased, neither had he a mind any more to search curiously to know what should befall him hereafter, but studied rather to inquire what was the good and acceptable will of God, for the beginning and perfecting of every good work. (*The Imitation of Christ*, Chapter 25, "Of the Zealous Amendment of Our Whole Lives").

It is a fair assumption with Ash Wednesday being soon upon

[†]   Written by dom Noah Moerbeek, CPMO

us that many, if not all of our readers, have already figured out what penances, mortifications, and spiritual exercises they intend to do during Holy Lent. Whatever additional burdens you have chosen for yourself to expiate your sins, I think it is a worthwhile endeavor to examine every part of our day and ask, "Is this work perfect?"

The thought of perfection is enough to make most of us shudder. Whether considered from strictly an objective point of view (perfecting the action) or a subjective point of view (perfecting the intention), our fallen natures and weak bodies resist the discipline under which we put ourselves.

If it was not so sad, it would be laughable that so many people in the devout Catholic subculture are so worried and guarded today about fasting too much. Those people who observe a technical rigor with their Lent are scorned, as if a person was incapable of fasting strictly and overcoming sin at the same time. "You know, you don't *have* to do that," they are scolded.

I admit there is a danger in such a thing, though I am not sure how frequently most approach that danger today. Yet it is a pitiable thing that we toss out the treasure we might store up in the kingdom during Lent with our meager penances by still allowing ourselves many sins and imperfections.

The Fathers both observed and preached rigorous fasts. They, too, saw the absurdity of giving up food only to endure in vices. Chrysostom said, "Fasting consists not in abstinence from food [only], but in a separation from sinful practices; since he who limits his fasting only to an abstinence from meats, is one who especially disparages it. Dost thou fast? Give me proof of it by thy works."

If I could extend a challenge to you for this Lent, I would suggest that you work on perfecting every good work. What do I mean? I mean the pursuing in your Lenten observance—side by side with your penance—a pure intention in the execution of your duties (i.e., those which are given to you by your state of life). For workers that means diligence in labor; for children, attention at study, etc. To sanctify those daily moments, those places where we are forced to spend so much time, and to focus on redeeming it rather than waiting for holiness to happen. In other words, sanctify your "trips in the car."

How can we sanctify our trips in the car? We must fill our cars with the Spirit of God. Pray the Rosary, listen (or sing along) to holy music, listen to Catholic audiobooks and the like. For those more advanced in spiritual things, perhaps sitting in silence, focusing on the presence of God. Do these things *in addition* to the prayers you already say, and the reading you already do. It would be going backwards to go from praying your Rosary on your knees to praying it just in the car; but it is redeeming the time to go from listening to the radio, to listening to St. Augustine. This does not mean that listening to music is bad, but rather that we can make progress when we choose something better and more pleasing to God.

People today are more likely to cease being your friend if you insult their favorite band than if you insult their religion. Our cars are oftentimes quite comfortable, people carefully select their music, and time in the car can be quite pleasant. It may be easy to fully give car time to God once in a while, but what about every day?

> Now shalt thou labor a little, and thou shalt find great rest, yea everlasting joy. If thou shalt remain faithful and zealous in labor, doubt not that God shall be faithful and bountiful in rewarding thee. (*Imitation of Christ*)

25

The Distraction of That One Sin

✤

W e all have that one sin. That one sin that we feel drags us down, oppresses us, and particularly embarrasses us. It is the one sin that we find ourselves confessing time and time again, much to our shame. We may believe that this sin and this sin alone stands between us and holiness. "If I could just get past this one sin, then I would truly be saintly," we tell ourselves. What the sin is exactly does not matter; it differs from person to person. For some it may be masturbation; for others, screaming at the children or talking down to the wife. Maybe it is using bad language at work or some similar accommodation with the mores of the world. Whatever the sin is, we have all had the experience. That one sin.

Maybe you have struggled with "that one sin" for many years. No matter how well other things are going in your life, you always returned to this one sin, as a dog to vomit. You feel profound embarrassment at having to keep coming back to confession every month and confessing the same thing; of course, the shame you feel is entirely in your head, a result of coming to terms with your own weakness rather than any condemnation laid upon you by the priest. Does it somehow occupy a central place in your life, in such a manner that you view it as the fundamental barrier between yourself and holiness? Is the entire focus of your thoughts on how bad this sin is and how succumbing to it keeps you down? Does this sin seem to keep you stuck in a rut?

I have been there before as well, brethren. But then one day the good Lord gave me a striking realization. Of course, this one sin was bad. Of course, like all sin, it separates us from God and, if not repented of, can lead to eternal death. Of course it needs to be overcome. But even so, preoccupation with this one particular sin is not helpful. In fact, such preoccupation can become a distraction. Excessive focus on the struggle with one particular sin keeps us distracted from the very real problems with other sins, to such a degree that a large part of our spiritual life gets shrouded in the darkness. This happens when one's spiritual focus is too myopic.

It is easy to focus on sins that are particularly embarrassing or that we fall into frequently. But there are other sins that are easy to overlook because, instead of being embarrassed by them, we want to justify them. Instead of feeling a sharp remorse after we commit them, we hardly notice we are perpetrating them because they come so natural to us. In my life, I noticed my preoccupation with my one sin had caused me to remain in ignorance about a festering anger and resentment growing in my heart towards certain individuals, in addition to other bad habits in several areas of my life.

In a sense, these other sins remain unknown to our conscience because we are too preoccupied on the one defect that troubles us most. We can even come to view ourselves as suffering from one and *only* one defect. This, of course, is a prideful position to be in—as if one suffers from only *one* sin and that's all! But it is also extremely dangerous. Gossip, resentment, and laziness can be difficult to discern because they feel so good. How pleasurable it is to remain in idleness rather than be industrious! After all, I've earned it, right? How easy it is to maintain resentment and anger against individuals whom we dislike. After all, if they weren't so contrary, stubborn, or irritating, I wouldn't have the problem. If I do have an aversion to them, it is their fault, right? How easy it is to stand around and gossip about people's affairs! I mean, I'm not speaking ill of them, I'm just keeping my friends informed about what's going on. And my motives all seem good. After all, I only mention all these things so you can remember to pray for them...

The excuses are manifold. But the point is that these sorts of sins get ignored because they are not sensational. They are not in the same category as, say, adultery or pornography or masturbation or out and out theft or violence, sins where you realize you have committed them immediately and can be immediately moved to penitence by a strong sense of shame or remorse. These sins can fester for years because they are deeper seated and are easier to justify. In this sense, they can be even more dangerous. What long term damage do I do to my soul by living in anger towards a certain person for twenty years? How many graces does that resentment choke up? How much of a drag would it be? How dangerous is a long-term disposition to laziness, especially in spiritual matters? These kinds of sins can be deadly in the long run, maybe more deadly than the one with which you are preoccupied.

This is where we must realize the diabolical element. Not only is it easy to be distracted by one particular sin which preoccupies us, but this distraction is actually a *diversion*; it is a tactic of the evil one to keep our eyes fixed on immediate problems while distracting us from long term trends. The devils make a very loud and obnoxious attack on our front door so that we will not notice them simultaneously undermining the foundations of our house.

What is the solution? How do we break out of the rut and stop ourselves from falling for this diversion? It is certainly not an acceptable solution to just start ignoring the one sin and focusing on the others. It is never a good idea to ignore *any* sin ultimately. We need to approach our spiritual life in a holistic way, fully understanding the way that the parts relate to the whole—that the different compartments we divide our life into are all connected. The sins I commit at work are related to the problems I have at home and vice versa; the carnal sins of the flesh I fall into so easily are related to other sins of pride.

In my particular case, I noted that the evil one seemed to be using my one sin to keep me distracted from several other more subtle problems I had. I therefore reversed the attack; I began to be much more introspective and active in my efforts to address the problems I had with anger, laziness, and gossip; but (and this is key), not simply switching my preoccupation from one sin to another, but with the intention of knowing that if I progressed in these areas I would progress across the board, and my other sin would be easier to deal with. I learned to examine my conscience more strictly, attempted certain virtues to counteract my bad habits, etc., and learned more about the way virtues and vices work, understanding that certain sins proceed from others.

I also decided that though my one sin was shameful, I was not going to let my spiritual life be defined by it. I would continue to work patiently against it, but I would also stop taking myself so seriously—stop fantasizing that I would be a saint without it, that it was my sole fault. In other words, I treated it like a sin, but like any other sin, neither attaching too much importance to it nor downplaying it.

Then, after a few months, I had a breakthrough: I realized that the one sin was very intimately connected with the problem with laziness, with lack of exertion. Laziness was the parent vice, and in working against the parent, I began to strike at the offspring. Soon, I noticed that I was committing my one sin much less. This got me excited, and I began to throw myself into the struggle with more resolve.

The sloth evaporated, and with it the despair. I realized I was not doomed to commit this one sin forever, that there was an end. Prayer intensified, the will was strengthened, and before I knew it I had not only improved across the board, but I had gone months without the one sin. Then the month became a year. As of today, it has been over five years since I have committed this sin.

There are other things to take into account as well; often we do not overcome a certain sin because of a fear of suffering, i.e., we are not willing to part with the occasion (person, place, thing) that prompts us to that sin, and hence we take only half measures. Rousing ourselves is part of realizing how sin is structured into our routines. We also must learn to love the combat necessary to overcome sin, to see it as a working out of God's grace in our lives.

All sin must be dealt with, but it is very necessary for us to understand what the structures of sin and the tactics of the evil one after. Sins and vices do not just spring up here and there with no relation to one another; individual sins result from vices, and vices, like virtues, have a certain structure—capital vices (the "deadly sins") serving as roots from which other sins branch off. It is a constant tactic of the enemy to keep us busy pruning the branches of the tree while leaving the roots intact. This happens whenever we get preoccupied with one particular sin to the exclusion of all others.

Whatever your one sin is, it can be overcome, so long as you can get a realistic grasp on the situation by identifying what "parent" vice is causing the sin and learn to view your "special" sin as just another sin—it should not be ignored, but it doesn't identify you either. There is hope. Ask God to show you the way.

26

The Untruth We All Profess

❧

If you are a Catholic striving after sanctity, you make a sincere effort to avoid all mortal sin and even venial sin. You certainly value truthfulness as a basic requirement for living a vibrant spiritual life and never intentionally tell lies or deceive others. Yet even so, there is one untruth I have learned that Catholics, even very pious, faithful Catholics, are guilty of telling. And they tell it time and time again, sometimes every day. We go on deceiving others with this untruth, sometimes deceiving ourselves as well. We do it repeatedly, sometimes to the same people. Most likely it is not intentional; we do not set out to be untruthful, but we become untruthful nonetheless. And this untruthfulness is not harmless; it is an untruth that can do grave harm to our own spiritual life and deprives others of very necessary graces. If not rectified, this habitual untruth can lead to a devastating habit of spiritual neglect. And yet, even then, even knowing this, we continue to do it.

Have you figured out what lie I am talking about, what untruth we habitually tell other people? Is it clear yet? What untruth am I talking about?

"I'll pray for you."

We sign up for prayer chains with pious intentions, then neglect to actually offer the prayers we have committed to. Many of us have all but tuned out the "prayer intentions" section in our parish bulletin. When in hearing about others' problems and calamities, we often sympathize and say, "I'll pray for you," but then when we do our rosaries and holy hours we are consumed with our own troubles—that is, if we manage to keep our minds from wandering totally. Yes, "I'll pray for you" is probably the biggest untruth we habitually perpetrate—surely the most well-intentioned untruth, but an untruth nonetheless.

Sometimes we realize our neglect in this area. Sometimes, as we are going through our evening rosary, we remember how we took our friend's hand and assured them of our prayers. Pricked with remorse over failing to pray for them, we will often retroactively add our friend's intention to the rosary we are just wrapping up, or maybe say a few extra Hail Mary's on their behalf. Such efforts, though better than nothing, signify our spiritual laziness when it comes to praying for others.

The mightiest prayer warriors of our faith were all great intercessors. They derived great spiritual benefit from pleading the causes of others, and their prayers were heard because of their great love. The great intercessors were not simply content to mention the names of their people before their rosaries; they deeply held the concerns of their people in their hearts, brought them lovingly before the Lord in rapt prayer, wept on their behalf before the altars, sometimes praying all night for them. St. Francis spent entire days fasting and praying for the brothers of his order; St. Monica wept and prayed for Augustine for years, and the heart of the great Doctor of the Church was softened for conversion by the tears of his mother's impassioned prayers. St. Padre Pio and St. John Bosco labored entire nights in spiritual combat for specific boys under their charge.

When we pray for others, our prayers should be passionate. In this way we allow divine charity to bridge the gap between our own life and needs and those of others. "For if there be first a willing mind, it is accepted according to that a man has, and not according to that he has not" (2 Cor. 8:12). If we take the initiative truly to reach out to God on behalf of another, to cherish them and their problems in our heart and bring them before God in prayer, God will take up our prayers and transfigure our disposition through Divine Charity, helping us love beyond what we thought capable and rendering our prayers fruitful and beautiful.

Part of this is simply committing to actually taking the time to pray—*really* pray—for the people who entrust their intentions to us. How can we ensure this happens? One of the great intercessors of the modern Church was Bl. Solanus Casey, the famous humble Capuchin friar of St. Bonaventure Monastery in Detroit. Bl. Solanus (d. 1957) was assigned the role of porter in the St. Bonaventure Monastery, a job which brought him into contact with all the troubled souls who came to the monastery seeking spiritual solace. After hearing their stories, he began noting their intentions in a small booklet, which he would take with him to adoration. He would use the book with its many names and intentions as a guide to his prayers, moving lovingly down the list and praying intently for each person on it.

As he did this over the years, he began to note that the prayers were being answered. This inspired Bl. Solanus to note not only the intentions in his book, but the dates they were answered. What great faith! Over the decades at St. Bonaventure Monastery, he cataloged thousands of prayers answered.

What if we were to adopt Bl. Solanus Casey's method? What if we were to carefully note the intentions people brought to us in a book, and keep this notebook among our treasured spiritual books we take with us to Adoration? What if we made a point to spend at least five minutes in impassioned, intentional, and focused prayer on each intention in our book, going down the list? And how would our faith be strengthened and our souls edified if we were to also record the answers to these prayers, creating an ongoing chronicle of God's goodness in the lives of those around us?

"I'll pray for you." Let us transform it from a platitude we say thoughtlessly to a core principle of our spiritual life.

27

With the Joy of Christ's
First Breath

❧

A most happy, blessed Easter to all of you who may be
reading this, whether you are Catholic or not. I pray for
the mercy and grace of our Lord to be with you abundantly
during this holy season, or whenever your eyes fall upon
these words.

This Easter marks the 19th Easter I have celebrated
as a Catholic. I remember receiving the sacred unction of
Confirmation all those years ago, taking the name Francis
in honor of the great saint of Assisi whose witness led me
to the Church. Last night, I watched a man and a woman
enter the Catholic Church at my parish's Easter Vigil.
Despite everything going on in the world, despite all the
darkness in the Church itself, there were still people who
heard the voice of the Bridegroom and followed Him into
His chambers, seeking the ark of salvation. One of the men
being confirmed even took the name Francis, just as I had
all those years ago.

At the time, I was a tad envious of those people. They
were likely blissfully unaware of a whole lot of things. To
use a tired cliché, they had not yet been "red pilled" to the
disaster in which Catholicism currently finds itself. There
are times when I wish I could take the proverbial "blue pill"
and forget about it all. Go back to believing all the modern

popes were flawless. To believing in the New Springtime. To thinking the documents of Vatican II were profound. To ignorantly thinking an okay Novus Ordo Mass represented 2,000 years of Tradition. To believing most of the bishops were good men, that scandal was due just "a few bad apples." To blaming the Church's public relations problems on media bias. To being moved to tears reading the *Catechism of the Catholic Church*. And yes, as I watched that man be confirmed as Francis, a part of me wished I could take a blue pill and forget it all. Does not the Proverb say, "He who increases in knowledge increases in sorrow" (Prov. 3:13)?

Nevertheless, "Restore unto me the joy of thy salvation," O Lord (Ps. 52:12); and "rejoice in the Lord always" (Phil. 4:4). Even though such thoughts tempt me from time to time, I have also reflected that my spiritual life is much better now than it was then. Back then I was restless, striving, tossed about by the wind. Now I feel much more solid, more at rest, more at peace, more grounded. And it is ironic because it doesn't seem to matter what goes on in the world and the Church; in a paradoxical sense, I found *more* peace the worse things got. Isn't that how trials work? They compel you to let go of your worldly understanding and cleave to the Lord. To have faith in Him. They purify your attachments, teaching you to trust in God alone. That's the way it works. Who ever said these trials would not come from or through the Church itself?

Going back to St. Francis, what originally drew me to him all those years was his radical sense of abandonment. Not just renunciation of worldly goods, but of worldly concerns. I'm sure Francis was well aware of papal corruption. Of clerical worldliness. Of priestly ineptitude. Of Christian hypocrisy. Of the darkness of the world and the power of evil. But he simply didn't focus on that. He focused on the cross of Christ, and therein he found perfect joy. Joy that enabled him to hug the leper on the road, or build San

Damiano stone after stone, or talk to a wolf or a bird in beautiful simplicity.

Where is faith lived out? I mean, *really?* There's only one possible space it can be lived out—*right where you are.* With the people who are right in front of you. In the circumstances you actually find yourself in. The chance to be a saint is right now. Will there be some sort of future restoration, some glorious triumph of Tradition? Who knows. But what I do know is that "now is the acceptable time of God's favor; today is the day of salvation" (2 Cor. 6:2). "Today, if you hear His voice, harden not your hearts" (Heb. 3:15). Yes, being a Catholic is hard, especially these days; some people I know have even thrown in the towel, to my great sadness. Their walk is their own. But for me, the older I get, the further I go, the more the Lord has helped me to focus on the here and now. And this has been a tremendous gift to my inner peace. I would rather be here where I am now than anywhere else.

You, too, friend. *Today* is your day. Have you hardened your heart? It is not that what's going on in the Church or in Rome doesn't matter; that stuff does matter—souls are being lost because of it, and a lot of people are going to have a very heavy judgment on the Day of the Lord on account of it. It is a problem, and as a Catholic it is *my* problem, in a sense. But in another sense, it is not, just as the corruption in Rome was not St. Francis's concern. But the leper in front of him *was* his concern. The avarice of some cardinal did not perturb him; the sin he discerned in his own heart did. His spiritual focus was ever trained on his own life and actions.

The great paradox, of course, is that by focusing so intensively on his own spiritual life, he did, in fact, end up reforming the Church. That was never his aim. But God did it through Him because that's how God is.

Even though it is tempting to want the blue pill, I have realized the Gospel *always* gives me a way out. I don't have to choose between being naively ignorant or red pilled and cynical. Just like St. Francis, I can choose joy. I can choose the joy that is in front of me every single day, always evident to those who have eyes to see, who, by the grace of God, have made their hearts like children. I can live in the joy of the Resurrection, with the clarity and freshness and radiance of the first breath in Christ's lungs when He stepped out of the tomb. Ah, what a joyful breath that must have been!

May that be my joy—the joy of Christ's first breath. The joy that is complete, that no man can taketh. And may it be yours as well, whomever you are and whatever life has dealt you.

28

A Miserable Cup of Coffee

❧

L ooking at passages from the Scriptures, the Fathers, and the lives of the saints, it is clear that there are varying degrees of sanctity a Christian is capable of obtaining. One degree is merely doing what is *acceptable* to God; i.e., not sinful. This may allow one to eek one's way into heaven with a detour through purgatory, but it does not constitute holiness in the strict sense. Another degree is doing the *good*, that is, orienting our life around God and making a sincere effort to be a good Catholic. Then there is the third degree, the way of *perfection*, which consists in denying attachments to this world in a heroic degree to attain sanctity above all else. Those who make progress in this way of perfection are saints in the most perfect sense of the word.

This concept of three stages is well-attested in tradition, whether speaking of the three conversions in the spiritual life, as does Fr. Garrigou-Lagrange in his classic book by the same name, or the three-fold path of Purgative, Illuminative, and Unitive ways, or the patristic idea of three levels of "reward" granted to confessors, virgins, and martyrs. There are differences between these variant concepts of course, but the idea of a three-fold progression in holiness is firmly rooted in Tradition.

Whichever schema we choose, the fundamental movement of the soul is preferring the good to the evil, then preferring the better to the good, and finally the best to the better. A person who has attained a high degree of sanctity understands the variations along this spectrum and always calls those seeking perfection to abandon all, even the good, for the sake of what is best. The saints are all different, but the one attribute they share is *abandonment*. This abandonment may look strange or harsh to those on the outside, almost as if they are denigrating things that are in themselves good—like a stable career, spousal love, a good reputation, etc.—but in fact, they recognize that the good can become the greatest obstacle to the best.

A classic example of this principle in practice comes from the life of St. Elizabeth Ann Seton (1775–1821). Mother Seton was a loving, tender woman, but she also was ardently devoted to God and had a sound Catholic sense of the hierarchy of goods. St. Elizabeth Ann Seton was a very careful guard over the spiritual lives of those entrusted to her care. If she saw a sister who did not go up to communion, she often inquired as to why. Once, a sister who did not go up to communion revealed to St. Elizabeth that she had not been feeling well and was a bit fatigued and so could not keep the Eucharistic fast.

"Mother," the sister said, "I felt a little weak, and took a cup of coffee before Mass."

"Ah, my dear child," said Mother Seton sternly, "how could you sell your God for a miserable cup of coffee?"[1]

Coffee, of course, is not intrinsically evil. Nor is there any mandate to receive communion every morning, not today, much less the early 19th century when frequent communions were less common. Furthermore, the sister stated that she was feeling weak, perhaps a tad sick. So she was certainly not in any sense morally "wrong" for taking a drink of coffee before Mass. Yet still, her act received a

---

[1]   Joseph I. Dirvin, C. M., *Mrs. Seton* (Emmitsburg, MD: Basilica of the National Shrine of St. Elizabeth Ann Seton, 1993), 342

seemingly harsh rebuke from Mother Seton, "How could you sell your God for a miserable cup of coffee?"

Of course, Mother Seton's admonishment was one of love, not of mere nitpicking. St. Elizabeth had a keen understanding of the hierarchy of goods; there is a spectrum of good, better, best, and that for those seeking perfection, the biggest enemy of the best is the good. Coffee is not bad; for many of us, it is an integral part of our daily routine. But when compared to God, it becomes a "miserable cup of coffee." Any worldly good becomes "miserable" when compared to the glory of God. A cup of coffee. Your career. Your apostolate. Even your family. "If any man come to me, and hate not his father, and mother, and wife, and children, and brethren, and sisters, yea and his own life also, he cannot be my disciple" (Luke 14:26). And those who have entered religious life have pledged themselves to seek these perfections with all possible zeal. Mother Seton's duty was to orient her sisters towards those perfections.

Again, we are not talking about things that are morally bad, but in choosing to forego things that are good in order to obtain those spiritual riches, stored up "where neither moth nor rust consumes and where thieves do not break in and steal" (cf. Matt. 6:20). But what would Mother Seton say to us today? How would she assess our own priorities? Are there goods in our own lives which, by the priority we give them, become "miserable" in that they keep us from achieving our highest in Him?

29

The Dark Mirror of Faith

❧

I often come across Catholics who are "wrestling" with something. They are trying to understand how God's benevolence can be reconciled with the evils in the world. They struggle sorting out what they believe on questions pertaining to evolution and the origin of things. They want to affirm the Church's claims about itself but are put off by the vices of the clergy. Living in a modern secular world, they try to delineate exactly how the Catholic faith should be lived out in terms of dress, habits, hobbies, etc. They agonize over what liturgy they should be attending. They struggle to find adequate political and economic expression of their beliefs within the current system. They labor to find meaning in the twists, turns, and disasters of their own lives. And so long as they cannot resolve these conflicts, they do not feel peace. They often experience a sense of disquiet; part of their faith seems incomplete, or on "hold" until they can resolve these intellectual struggles. They feel profoundly that they must "settle" these matters to attain tranquility.

The life of faith will bring forth many such struggles, and this is unavoidable. But God wants us to have peace, even in the midst of struggle. "Peace I leave with you; my peace I give to you; not as the world gives do I give to you" (John 14:27). His peace is meant to be an abiding peace;

not a peace "as the world gives" that is taken away as soon as conflict emerges. We are meant to have peace, even amid the "wrestling" that is inherent in faith. What kind of peace would Christ offer if we were thrown into turmoil every time we encountered something we couldn't reconcile? Clearly, our Lord means for the peace of our faith to be maintained even during uncertainty. But how can we accomplish this?

To do this, remember that *you do not need to resolve your difficulties in order to maintain faith.*

Let us recall three fundamental realities about the nature of faith: it is trusting, provisional, and imperfect, considering each in turn.

Faith is a kind of knowledge, but unlike empirical knowledge (which is based on experience), faith is *based on trust* in someone else. So even though we can have certainty grounded in the trustworthiness of the one in whom we believe, it is not the same kind of certainty that comes with empirical experience (what the Bible calls "knowledge"). The way we "know" something through faith is thus fundamentally different than the way we "know" things through empirical experience. So first, we need to recognize that difference and be comfortable with it. The certitude of faith will never "feel" like the certitude you have about empirical knowledge, and that is okay. It's not meant to feel the same.

Second, recall that faith is *provisional*. It is a temporary state that is meant to pass away. Faith, hope, and charity we abide in here and now, but in heavenly glory, faith and hope pass away; only charity then remains. Faith and hope are proper to people who are still "on the journey," *viators*, those who are pilgriming here below towards "that city whose builder and maker is God" (Heb. 11:10). Faith gives us a semblance of what we are doing and where we are going, but it is inferior to the knowledge that will come. Faith is like looking at a map to try to get yourself to a city; heaven is actually being there, standing in the midst of the heavenly

Jerusalem with your feet planted firmly and irrevocably on its golden causeways.

Because faith is provisional, it is *imperfect*. Not imperfect in the sense that anything is lacking in the formulations of faith, but in the sense that faith alone does not give us the sense of finality that we all crave. It is something with which we are *meant* to wrestle. Faith offers us a broader view than what we could otherwise have, but it is a view through the mist, partially obscured. "When the perfect comes, the imperfect will pass away. When I was a child, I spoke like a child, I thought like a child, I reasoned like a child; when I became a man, I gave up childish ways. For now we see in a mirror dimly, but then face to face. Now I know in part; then I shall understand fully, even as I have been fully understood" (1 Cor. 13:10–12). The experience of faith, even for St. Paul, was "seeing in a mirror dimly." There is always going to be a sense of imperfection, a deep yearning, a wrestling, a sense of "not yet-ness" about our faith. A wandering about in the murky dusk of existence, struggling to come into the brilliance of daylight.

Even if we are occasionally graced with periods of clarity and resolution, there will always ultimately be a kind of tension so long as we are in the flesh. Why is it like this? Because that is the nature of faith; it is the difference between being on a journey and arriving at your destination. We cannot demand the fulfillment of the arrival when we are yet on the road. And, if by some miracle of God, we had all the knowledge and finality and certainty we could possibly desire here and now, what incentive would we have to grow ourselves? Aristotle once observed that "all men by nature desire to know." It is the curiosity of life, the unquenchable thirst to "get to the bottom of things" that propels us, drives us on towards new adventures, new conquests, and ever greater horizons. There is a cliché that "the real treasure is the friends you make along the way;" goofy as this cliché is, there is a kernel of truth in it: what matters is how we comport ourselves on the journey. The effort yields its own rewards. It is not about how many talents you are given (cf. Matt. 25:14–30), it's not about whether you ever attain the great intellectual or moral or spiritual synthesis you are struggling to birth into existence; it's about walking, one foot after another, towards that luminous horizon with the sun on your face.

Abraham was the father of faith; he was called out and sojourned into a foreign land in search of what he knew not, based on promises he never lived to see fulfilled. Likewise, all of us who live in faith must sojourn in a strange land. That is the essence of being a *believer*. You must grow comfortable with the sojourn, with the provisional nature of the journey.

What does this mean concretely?

It is obviously a good and praiseworthy thing to seek out knowledge, to learn, and grow in understanding. It is good to seek as much certainty as we can get. But moderation in all things—you must also acknowledge your limits; there are some things you may never reconcile, and others that may take a long time to understand. This state of "not knowing" is okay and should be embraced. Understand that it is a normal part of faith to grapple with something. Perhaps it is part of our western rationalist bias that makes us feel like our faith will be stronger once we have sorted everything out intellectually, once we can "reason it all out" like some sort of engineering schematic. I challenge you to consider backing away from that premise: you don't need to take a position on everything; you don't need to understand how the pieces of something all fit together; you don't need to reconcile every contradiction; you don't need to see clearly or have all the answers. Get comfortable with not knowing. The beginning of wisdom is admitting you do not know as much as you think; learn to say, "I am still wrestling with this; I don't know what I think about it. If it please

God, someday I will." That's a perfectly valid response to the conundrums that faith presents to us. To have faith is to wrestle with things; *accept that.*

I can foresee some critiquing this concept by saying that I suggest we just believe blindly even though our mind can no longer assent; that I am telling people just to stuff their difficulties and boldly proclaim CREDO! despite their faltering heart. This is not so. Faith is fundamentally an act of trust, and if that trust has been so compromised as to become unsustainable, then faith is impossible, and it would be wrong and cruel to tell someone to simply ignore it. I am, however, suggesting that those of us who have faith give up thinking that we need to cross every jot and tittle; let go of the idea that being a strong believer means working out all the answers intellectually. Learn to rest in not knowing. You will not be denied heaven because you did not have a fully worked out intellectual synthesis of some disputed issue. If you find yourself in those moments of "wrestling," acknowledge the struggle, embrace it, and offer your ignorance to God.

"All I have written is like straw," said St. Thomas Aquinas after experiencing a vision of the Divine. No matter how brilliant we are, how much we think we know, or how hard we work to educate ourselves, we are all "seeing in a mirror dimly," as St. Paul says. The dimness may be frustrating at times, but it is part of faith. An essential part. We should learn to take comfort in that and embrace the tension.

30

The Relation of Gluttony and Lust

❧

The widespread dominion of lust, with all its attendant sins, is one the most serious crises facing the Catholic Church in the modern world. The extent to which the scourge of pornography has penetrated the Christian world is well documented. Whereas once upon time men needed to make a special trip to an adult bookstore in order to purchase pornographic materials, the advent of the Internet has made an unlimited abyss of pornography available anywhere there is an Internet connection. In 2008, the evangelical publication *Christianity Today* featured the results of a study that suggested as many as 50 percent of Christian men have looked at porn recently. One Protestant pastor, skeptical of the statistic, polled his own congregation and found the result was 60% within the past year and 30% within the past 30 days.[1]

Even if we can thankfully say that we are part of the 50% who have not viewed pornography either ever or in the recent past, how much more prevalent is masturbation? Though the statistics are harder to come by here, the evidence seems to suggest that regular masturbation among Christian males across denominational lines is somewhere around 87%; some estimates place this as high as 95%.

---

[1] https://www.christianitytoday.com/ct/2008/march/20.7.html

And even if we could possibly boast that we are among the 5-13% of Christian men who do not practice regular masturbation, how often do we struggle with impure thoughts or cast our gaze too long at immodest images we see as we go about our day? The battle against lust sometimes seems all-encompassing, and every victory only a temporary gain until the next fall.

Some pastors have chosen to ignore the uncomfortable subjects of pornography and masturbation; some have tried to make a truce with lust, like evangelical icon Dr. James Dobson, who famously taught that masturbation in Christian boys was "not much of an issue with God" and should not be discouraged.[2]

But, to their credit, there have also been many pastors who have spoken out vehemently against the vice of lust, including use of pornography and masturbation. Yet, even among orthodox Catholic parishes where these sins are preached against and where recourse to the confessional is frequent, there is still a grave problem. Many men in perfectly sound, orthodox parishes that foster healthy spirituality still struggle desperately with lust—and in many cases, it is a losing struggle. Why does this seem to be one battle that Catholic men have such a difficulty winning?

We can of course point to the culture, to the absolute inundation of immodest images in our society. We could also make a case that the ease of accessibility of such images greatly increases the likelihood that men will access them. But these answers alone are not sufficient; sins of lust do not just "happen" to people; they require formal cooperation. Nobody "falls" into looking at pornography, as if they were wandering along minding their own business and just tripped into it. The abundance of pornographic material and the ease of accessing it certainly make it easier for one

---

[2]   James Dobson, "Challenges in the Teen Years: Masturbation," Article, Focus on the Family, at: http://www.focusonyourchild.com/

to sin with less effort, but it does not explain why so many Christians seemed predisposed to commit these sins in the first place.

The answer, I believe, is that too many Catholics, even orthodox, traditional Catholics, are living unmortified lives. Despite fidelity to the Magisterium and a regular sacramental life, they have not "put to death the deeds of the flesh" (Rom. 8:13) through penance and prayer. Masturbation and pornography are specific issues, but they arise from the general problem of living an unmortified life.

Lust is nothing other than disordered, immoderate sexual desire. Sexual desire is good and natural; lust is a perversion of this desire through excess. Because it deals with excess with regards to bodily pleasure, we may rightly understand out sexual appetite to be governed by the virtue of temperance. According to St. Thomas, "temperance signifies a certain temperateness or moderation, which reason appoints to human operations and passions" (STh, II-IIQ. 141 Art. 2). Temperance consists of moderation in the use of our passions and created goods. In order to win the battle against lust, therefore, one must possess the virtue of temperance to be able to moderate our sexual desire.

In general, virtues and vices are coextensive with a person's entire character. This means if a person is immoderate in any aspect of their life, they are much more likely to be immoderate in other areas as well. A man who is wasteful with his money will most likely be wasteful with other things, such as his time. An individual who practices justice with regards to his family and acquaintance will most likely be just with others as well (co-workers, employees, etc.). Because virtues and vices are habits that form our character, they tend to cut across the different aspects of our lives in their effects.

To bring this back to lust: lust is a problem with temperance, and if we are intemperate with regards to our sexual desires, it is likely that we are intemperate in other areas, too. But the flip side of this is that, if we can identify and rectify the other areas of our lives in which we find problems with moderation, we are in a much stronger position to attack the vice of lust.

It is my personal opinion (and experience) that there is a profound correlation between lust and gluttony. I suspect persons who struggle with lust exercise little restraint on what they eat and drink. Gluttony, of course, is the immoderate intake of food and drink; lust, the immoderate desire of sexual pleasure. Both vices are connected, because immoderation with regards to food tends to enslave us to our basic instincts. When we once find ourselves giving in to our base instincts with regards to the bodily pleasure that we get from eating food, it is very difficult to avoid giving in to the pleasure of other bodily desires as well.

Let us be clear: I am not saying all people who struggle with lust are gluttons, nor am I speculating as to how much food or drink one needs to consume to be a glutton. I merely point out that issues of temperance tend to stand or fall together; one is either a temperate person, or one is not. The ancient authors, both pagan and Christian, have noted this specific connection between gluttony and lust. St. Jerome said, "The eating of flesh, and drinking of wine, and fullness of stomach, is the seed-plot of lust" (*Ad Jovinian*, 2.7). St. John Climacus said, "To be gluttonous, yet expect to be chaste, is to wish to extinguish fire with oil" (*Ladder of Divine Ascent*, 14). It matters not whether the object of our desire is food or sexual pleasure: when we do not mortify our bodily instincts, we become immoderate people and fail in any struggle that requires temperance.

Fine and good, but how does this help us combat lust? Because it is generally easier to moderate our intake of food than to break habits of sexual sin, it is my opinion that any serious attempt to break free from the vice of lust should begin with a general resolution to be moderate in all things pertaining to the body, especially food and drink. Spiritual power is unleashed when we mortify our desires and bring our prayers to the Lord when fasting. Besides the grace given us through fasting, it teaches us to practice bodily discipline and subject the desires of our body to the dictates of reason. He who is moderate in food and drink and practices regular fasting will grow in grace, cultivate the virtue of temperance, and find himself much better equipped to enter into combat against lust. There will still be a struggle, but the constant failures and setbacks that characterized earlier efforts will now give way to real and enduring victories.

For those in pastoral ministries, it is important not only to preach against the common vices of masturbation and pornography, but to preach and exemplify a mortified life, encouraging parishioners to fast and do penance. Trying to encourage people to chastity without teaching them mortification will be fruitless; those who have not developed the virtue of temperance will always be too spiritually weakened to fight lust, which is a very powerful enemy.

This is the way of the saints and fathers: moderation in all things, especially food and drink, make possible the moderation of sexual desire. But immoderation in food and drink leads to immoderation in our sexual desires.

31

"I Know That My Redeemer Lives"

❧

On this day we celebrate the Resurrection of our Lord Jesus Christ. The Resurrection is the greatest miracle and the principal testimony to the truth of our Lord's teaching, for, as St. Paul says, "If Christ be not raised, your faith is in vain; you are still in your sins" (1 Cor. 15:17). This is a potent reminder that it is not merely the crucifixion of Christ that saves us; our salvation is incomplete without His resurrection to glory. Jesus was "put to death for our trespasses and *raised for our justification*" (Rom. 4:25). His rising also serves as a pledge that we, too, shall be raised to life again, adoring God forever in our glorified flesh. Christ is "the first fruits of those who have fallen asleep. For as by a man came death, by a man has come also the resurrection of the dead. For as in Adam all die, so also in Christ shall all be made alive. But each in his own order: Christ the first fruits, then at his coming those who belong to Christ" (1 Cor. 15:20–24).

"The Son of Man is going to be delivered into the hands of men. They will kill him, and after three days he will rise. But they did not understand what he meant and were afraid to ask him about it" (Mark 9:31–32). Christ spoke plainly of the Resurrection to His disciples ahead of time, but the meaning of His words was veiled from them. The reason for this is uncertain; perhaps God delib-

159

erately obscured this truth from their minds, or perhaps they misunderstood through a defect in their own natural faculties. Whatever its cause, the Resurrection remained indiscernible to them before the fact. Thus, the death of Christ shattered their imaginings; the finality of the crucifixion must have made their squabbles about who would be the greatest in the Kingdom of Heaven seem childish and naïve. We can imagine what disappointment they must have had. A hint of this disillusionment can be heard in the voice of the nameless disciples Christ encountered on the road to Emmaus after the Resurrection: telling Him about the events surrounding the Crucifixion, they say, "we *had* hoped that he was the one who was going to redeem Israel" (Luke 24:21), the pluperfect "had hoped" signifying that they had once hoped, but now hoped no longer.

The Resurrection, then, was not a foregone conclusion to the disciples. We may presume the Blessed Virgin Mary to have nurtured this hope in her Immaculate Heart, but for the rest of His followers, we can assume they were as dejected as those Christ met on the Emmaus road. The Gospel of John tells us that after the Crucifixion, Peter and the other disciples returned to Galilee and went back to their lives as fishermen (John 21:1–3); this is not the sort of behavior we'd expect from men who were anticipating an imminent Resurrection of their Lord.

How glorious and life-changing, then, must have been the realization that the Lord had risen indeed! How excited Peter must have been when, hearing Christ's voice from the shore, he leaped from his boat into the sea to swim to His Master. How stupefied the disciples must have been as they sat around the fire on the beach in stunned silence watching the Resurrected Messiah munching on roasted fish. But if these moments were astonishing, it was only the apparent finality of His death that rendered them so. For had He not truly died, His sudden reappearance would not have been as stupendous. Suppose Christ had not died, but merely been wounded and escaped; His reappearance would have been welcome, to be sure, but not astounding and certainly not life-altering.

The Lord's ultimate demonstration of His power did not prevent suffering; it came rather *after* the evil had been done. This is the locus of the Resurrection for us as well. There is no rising to life if there first be no death. For every Christian, this entails a "dying to sin" so we can rise to "newness of life" (Rom. 6:4). This is the spiritual Resurrection that every Christian undergoes. But all of us work through many smaller "resurrections" throughout our lives. I am speaking of the "death" we all experience whenever we suffer in any sense. The sufferings we undergo are manifold: abuse by others, destructive behavior from ourselves, or agonies of nature. God's power to "deliver us from evil" does not often free us from the experience of these things; it turns them to good. The only way out is through; this is the lesson of the Resurrection. In a sense, every little victory of grace is a resurrection: when I finally divest myself the burden of resentment towards someone who has wronged me, that is a resurrection. When I overcome a bad habit, that is a resurrection. When I speak a word of comfort to a wounded spirit, or deny myself some pleasure for the good of my soul, or find God in the deepest midst of my suffering and ignorance, these are little resurrections. But, like the Resurrection of Christ, we find they do not come save in the *aftermath* of some chaos, some evil, some catastrophe.

Whether we like it or not, we are all handed burdens in this life, and the challenge of our existence is to rise above them, that in doing so we may know ourselves better and conform ever more closely to the image of God. Nature establishes the parameters of our existence, but we are to transcend what nature has given us. This is the function of grace—to elevate our nature, ennoble us, transfigure us into something greater than we could have ever become on our own. This is the hope of the Resurrection, both the "little" resurrections of daily life, and the grand Resurrection, when we shall see God. But it is a "hope against hope" (Rom. 4:18), born from death, like a seed falling to the earth sprouts into new life. And when that fresh life blossoms into glory, we shall see, on that day when all that is hidden shall be manifest (cf. Matt. 10:26; Luke 8:17), how every tear and heartache and loss was but another stone into the spiritual temple we are all called to become (1 Pet. 2:5); scars gilt in gold, trials become gems, wounds turned to radiant light.

Thus, with Job, I say, "I know that my Redeemer lives, and at last he will stand upon the earth; and after my skin has been thus destroyed, then from my flesh I shall see God, whom I shall see on my side, and my eyes shall behold, and not another" (Job 19:25–27).

> *Restore our fortunes O' Lord,*
> *like the watercourse in the Negev*
> *May those who sow in tears*
> *reap with shouts of joy!*
> *He that goes forth weeping,*
> *bearing the seed for sowing,*
> *shall come home with shouts of joy*
> *carrying their sheaves (Psalm 126:4–6).*

32

True and False Dark Nights

❧

There is a rich tradition in the West of describing the progress of the soul along the path to God in terms of stages of development, with certain characteristics proper to each stage. St. Teresa of Avila famously spoke of seven "mansions" corresponding to different levels of spiritual attainment; others divide the spiritual life into three phases: purgative, illuminative, and contemplative. Medieval mystics such as Robert Grosseteste, Julian of Norwich, and the author of the *Cloud of Unknowing*, followed the tradition of Pseudo-Dionysius and took an apophatic approach to their theology, viewing the ascent toward God as a stripping away of assumptions and images about God in an attempt to contemplate the divine essence itself.

All these approaches have merit, and we should probably not insist on adhering to one too closely; they are all ultimately subjective expressions of what particular souls have experienced. Even if these experiences have been quite common in Church history, God ultimately works with each soul in a unique manner. No two souls take the same journey, even though all souls who seek God seek the same end. These descriptions are meant to be pedagogical, teaching the devotee what to expect on the way to holiness. They are not doctrines that we must insist on to the exclusion of other conceptual frameworks.

That being said, that does not mean there is not some commonality across mystical experiences. Most of the progressions described in the mystical writings of the Church, East and West, center on a particular shift in experience from the intellect to the affections—from the head to the heart. For example, in the West, meditation is commonly recommended as a sort of prayer for beginners in the spiritual life. Meditation consists in taking a certain episode of sacred history or truth of the faith and holding it before the mind's eye, drawing out different levels of meaning, making pious resolutions, and dwelling on the implications of the truths of what we are meditating on. It is primarily an intellectual activity utilizing the imagination.

Similarly, the Eastern tradition places great emphasis on the Jesus Prayer, intentionally choosing a particular expression and repeating it while meditating on a specific element of the Faith. This is, again, an active, intellectual work that depends on human activity to open oneself up to the action of the divine.

But in both traditions, there is a transition that occurs at a certain point. In meditation, one eventually moves to contemplation, while in the Eastern tradition, the Jesus Prayer as an active repetition is supposed to yield to a more passive spirit of contemplative prayer. In both cases, the movement is from an active to a passive sort of prayer, from a field in which human activity predominates to one in which the soul is more responsive to the graces God wishes to bestow upon it. This transition cannot be forced; it does not yield to human effort. It may come on a soul suddenly, or gradually over many years, or perhaps never at all. No matter what schema we use to describe the transition, we get to a place where God is the dominant agent, and the soul must be docile before Him.

This transition can be painful and disorienting. In some mystical traditions (most notably the Carmelite tradition exemplified by St. John of the Cross), the movement into these higher degrees of spirituality is accompanied by a painful episode that is known as a "dark night." The dark night is typically described as a period of deprivation, where the sensations, pious aspirations, consolations, and happy feelings that accompanied the individual in the lower stages of the spiritual life are withdrawn. This process of the dark night is part of the larger transition from the "head to the heart" that God affects in the spiritual life of docile souls.

It is common knowledge that the dark night exists for the purpose of drawing souls closer to God, but why, specifically, is this the case? Why *must* a soul experience this deprivation of consolation in order to progress?

In this life, faith infused with charity is the only way a person can truly gain access to God in prayer. But when we begin, our faith and charity are weak and need to be propped up with other things: mental images, pious thoughts, spiritually pleasant feelings, imagination, etc. These are all objectively good; no matter how far we advance in the spiritual life, these will always have a certain place. But these things can never attain to God without a corresponding increase in faith, which is the key to prayer and union with the divine. The strengthening of faith we require to truly commune with God can only come about in a state of detachment, just as a person on crutches does not return to full use of their leg until the crutches are discarded and the muscles can be worked without the aid of the crutch. Similarly, growth in faith necessary to put a person into closer union with God requires that pious feelings, divine consolations, and the ability to approach Him through reason be set aside. This setting aside of all the active, human-based elements of the spiritual life is why persons in the dark night feel so incredibly helpless. Yet the dark night is extremely enriching, because by it, faith is strengthened, and prayer is transformed into a mutual exchange of love.

None of this is new to anyone who has even read a little bit of Catholic mystical theology, but it is something that is sadly misunderstood. There are plenty of counterfeit dark nights out there: experiences that people believe to be a dark night but are actually something other. For example, the dark night must be distinguished from a "period of dryness." All believers experience periods of dryness occasionally, during which prayer is difficult and spiritual consolations seem to be removed. This is what St. Ignatius refers to as the time of "desolation." These periods are usually briefer and are universal to all believers. These stretches of desolation can be used by God, or they can be inflicted by the evil one—God will typically use a period of desolation to turn someone towards Him, while the devil's desolation is characterized by confusion and wavering in resolutions. A spiritually mature believer needs to be able to discern these cyclic periods of dryness from the greater "dark night" that the saints speak about. In other words, you are not "going through a dark night" just because you are spiritually dry or having a hard time.

Furthermore—and probably more common—we cannot mistake true dark nights with periods of confusion or disorientation that arise due to our own sinful activities. For example, about fifteen years ago, I experienced a profound period of dryness and dissatisfaction that lasted for about two years. Prayer was very difficult. I seemed to be making no progress in my spiritual life and had a very challenging time focusing on God. In my own limited understanding of things at the time, I wondered if I was experiencing the dark night of the saints. What I did not consider was that I never prayed the Rosary, seldom went to Adoration, read the Bible only infrequently, attended Mass only on Sundays, and nurtured several bad habits and personal sins that I was unwilling to make the effort to overcome. In this case, was my dryness and difficulties really due to some dark night?

Were they not rather due to my lukewarmness? Thank God I was roused from that slumber!

A true dark night comes not to souls who are tepid, but to those who are fervent and burning with charity. This is why it is so distressing for them, precisely because they are typically so inflamed with zeal for our Lord that the deprivation of His consolations is devastating to them.

It has become, in a certain sense, fashionable to speak of dark nights. People discuss their spiritual lives far too openly, and everyone who experiences some momentary setback in prayer or some cyclic lack of initiative wistfully speculates to their friends or posts on social media that they are suffering a dark night. Dark nights are not fashionable. They are not something casually discussed, and they are not something that come to those whose pursuit of God is not relentless; even among those who do pursue Him relentlessly may never pass through it. They are extremely distressing to the souls who undergo them, and even souls of exemplary holiness and clarity of mind may not understand what is happening to them.

If we feel ourselves in a period of dryness or desolation, rather than speculating about if we have been sufficiently holy to merit undergoing the trial of the dark night, let us turn to the much more practical advice of St. Ignatius of Loyola: Consider that the dryness you experience is due to your own apathetic practice of the Faith. If you have noticed the dryness, however, God may make use of it to prod you on to a more fervent practice of the Faith. The fact that you recognize that you are dry is itself a grace. Ask God to bring you where He wants you to be and assent to whatever means He chooses to do this.

If you are already fervent in your faith, moving from good to better in the service of God, as St. Ignatius says, the dry spell may come from the evil one, who tries to place obstacles in the way of perfection. St. Ignatius calls this state "desolation." What can be done when this happens?

If you are in a state of desolation, do not make any changes to your spiritual routine. It is best to stay firm in our disciplines and resolves, focusing instead upon overcoming the desolation through prayer and meditation. Patience and fidelity to God are necessary here. Maintain faithfulness to the resolutions you made in the light. Changing your plan in the dark is never helpful because the desolation clouds your judgment. It will pass.

Besides our own slothfulness and tepidity, St. Ignatius says we sometimes go through periods of desolation because God wants to test us and try our faith, or because God wants to reveal to us our true state without the aid of His grace.

These periods of desolation are natural to all believers and are distinct from the dark night that is spoken of by the mystics and vouchsafed only to souls who have made exceptional progress in holiness. It is good to understand this and fortify oneself during a period of fruitful prayer and consolation by thinking how one will handle the desolation which will inevitably come.

If we made ourselves more familiar with these basic principles of spiritual life, we would do very well indeed. Through the successful navigation of these cycles of consolation-desolation, we in fact slowly come to master our spiritual life by God's grace and understand the movement of the Spirit. Thus, growing stronger, we eventually do come to the stage where our spiritual focus must shift from the head to the heart, and we may, in fact, undergo the dark night. But if we have not mastered handling our periodic desolations, what will we do when God's consolations are utterly removed during that time of darkness?

Mysticism may be mysterious, but there is an inner logic to it, and without proper discipline and ascesis, we can't even get past our own periodic desolations, let alone the true dark night.

33

Despair and Presumption

❧

"**O** Israel, hope in the Lord, now and forever more" (Ps 131:3). The *Catechism of the Catholic Church* defines hope as "the confident expectation of divine blessing and the beatific vision of God; it is also the fear of offending God's love and of incurring punishment" (CCC 2090). Most of us are familiar with despair and presumption as two sins against hope; presumption claims to have already laid hold of something that we do not yet fully possess, while despair leads us to believe it is impossible to ever possess it. The object of hope is a good which is difficult but possible to obtain—in our case, eternal life. Despair sins against hope by making something possible out to be impossible, while presumption sins against hope by making certain what is merely possible. Let us look at each of these sins in greater detail, using the golden wisdom of St. Thomas Aquinas to find our way.

First, we shall consider despair. St. Thomas defines despair as essentially an appetitive movement in the soul corresponding to a wrong or evil opinion about God; namely, that He will not forgive repentant sinners (II-II, q. 20, art. 1). Further, he teaches that despair is the most grievous of all sins, because by despairing of ever partaking in God's goodness, the sinner, in a certain manner, damns himself while he is yet living. Hence, though admitting that other sins may be objectively more grievous (such as unbelief and hatred of God), Aquinas says that from a subjective viewpoint, no sin is more deadly to us than despair:

> From our point of view, then, despair is more danger-
> ous, since hope withdraws us from evils and induces
> us to seek for good things, so that when hope is
> given up, men rush headlong into sin, and are drawn
> away from good works (II-II, q. 20, art. 3).

This is why despair is traditionally considered the unforgiv-able sin, a sin against the Holy Ghost, in that by refusing to admit God's mercy, the sinner makes it impossible for grace to work in him. This is why it is so dangerous.

St. Thomas also teaches that despair commonly arises from spiritual sloth (although interestingly enough, he also says lust can lead to despair). This is because despair sees the effort needed to attain the good as too arduous, too difficult to attain, and hence ends up denying that its attainment is possible. Because it sees spiritual effort as too arduous, it is based on spiritual sloth.

It follows, then, that the best remedy of despair is the contrary virtue of diligence, by which we demonstrate zeal, integrity, and effort in our spiritual undertakings.

Presumption is related to despair in that, as despair despises the Divine Mercy, so presumption despises the Divine Justice (II-II, q. 21, art. 1). Like despair, it is also a sin against the Holy Ghost. St. Thomas says:

> As to the hope whereby a man relies on the power
> of God, there may be presumption through immod-
> eration, in the fact that a man tends to some good
> as though it were possible by the power and mercy
> of God, whereas it is not possible, for instance, if a
> man hope to obtain pardon without repenting, or
> glory without merits. This presumption is, properly,
> the sin against the Holy Ghost, because, to wit, by

presuming thus a man removes or despises the assistance of the Holy Spirit, whereby he is withdrawn from sin (II-II, q. 21, a. 1).

Presumption is thus a sin by being an immoderate excess of hope, whereby a man presumes to possess eternal salvation prematurely. While noting its relation to despair, St. Thomas also teaches that it is not as grave as despair: because of His infinite goodness, it is more proper to God to have mercy and spare than it is to punish. In that the sin of despair denies God's fundamental attribute of mercy, it is a greater offense against Him than presumption, which merely takes the attribute of mercy to an immoderate degree (II-II, q. 21, art. 2).

While despair arises from sloth, presumption arises from vainglory, inasmuch as it is prideful to assume that God would never punish or exclude us regardless of our sins. Thus the way to combat presumption is by exercising humility.

It is, however, not sufficient to simply be able to define these sins. The devil, our adversary, is not only cunning at what temptations he attacks us with, but he is very cunning as to *when* he deploys certain attacks. We must develop an ability to identify attacks of despair and presumption and rebut them.

For example, common sense tells us that when we are doing well in our spiritual lives, we should be extraordinarily humble, lest we begin to attribute our success to our own efforts or fail to rely on God's grace. Knowing this, the devil is very keen to tempt us with thoughts of presumption when we are in a state of grace. "I had good prayer time last night; I don't need to do it tonight." "My spiritual life has really been going good lately; I'm going to go easy on myself for Lent." "I just went to Mass the other day; I'm going to sleep in today." "It's only a venial sin; you can't go to hell for venial sin." And right before we commit a sin, "I'll just go to Confession on Saturday..."

The attacks can be very subtle, often mixing truth with falsehood. But the crux of the matter is this: It is precisely when we should be practicing humility that the devil will tempt us with presumption—and this is when we are in a state of grace.

If the devil's attack works, we commit a serious sin. He wins. But that is only part of the strategy. Having gotten us to sin, the attack now changes. Whereas in grace we had immoderate confidence in God's mercy, now in a state of sin the devil wants us to despair of His mercy. "You did that again!" "You will never get over this sin. You'll struggle with it till the day you die." "God will never forgive you for that. God wants to damn you to hell." Just when we should be having the greatest confidence in God's mercy, the devil wants us to despair of it.

And, if he can get us to despair, he wins, and our soul may be lost. Now we see why, though despair and presumption are both sins against hope, despair is worse. Presumption is used as a tactic simply to get us to the point of despair; but despair in the end game, because one who has given way to despair has damned himself even while he lives. That is how the devil wins.

But "we are not ignorant of his devices" (2. Cor. 2:11). When we are doing well, or in a state of grace, let us remember to dispose our souls and minds in humility. Perhaps we are doing good. It is by God's grace, and if we have not fallen, let us not be reckless, but remember how many times we have fallen in the past. How many good resolutions have come to naught! How many promising beginnings derailed! Therefore, apply yourself with humble diligence to the things of the Spirit and remember that people—and angels—more spiritually advanced than you have fallen. "Do not be deceived; God is not mocked. Whatever a man sows, that also shall he reap" (Gal. 6:7). Remember that God is just.

But if you do fall and commit grave sin, then is the time to throw yourself upon God's mercy. God's mercy is infinite. It endures forever, as the Psalmist says (cf. Ps 136). God knows your frailties. He knows your struggles, and if you turn to Him in repentance and with a sincere desire to amend, He will extend mercy to you, forgive you, and restore you. "If we confess our sins to Him, He is faithful and just to forgive us our sins and to cleanse us from all wickedness" (1 John 1:9). Remember that God is merciful.

Satan's attack is a fundamental inversion of how our dispositions ought to be at given times. If we practice humility at all times and remember to throw ourselves on God's mercy when we fall, we can insulate ourselves against the deadly attacks of the evil one and persevere until the end.

34

Viators Seeking Perfection

🌼

For two millennia the evangelical counsels of poverty, chastity, and obedience have continued to draw faithful men and women into spiritual solitude and contemplation for the end of the perfection of the soul. Endless treatises from the *Life of Antony* to letters of Augustine to the *Dialogues* of St. Gregory the Great and the *Ecclesiastical History* of St. Bede have extolled the glories of the religious life. This manner of living has been instrumental in leading Catholics to seek perfection through the evangelical counsels. This continues today; the *Catechism* speaks about the perpetual fruit borne by observance of the evangelical counsels:

> From the God-given seed of the counsels a wonderful and wide-spreading tree has grown up in the field of the Lord, branching out into various forms of the religious life lived in solitude or in community. Different religious families have come into existence in which spiritual resources are multiplied for the progress in holiness of their members and for the good of the entire Body of Christ (CCC 917).

The purpose of entering religious life is "progress in holiness." Those who seek this progress are seeking nothing less than Christian perfection, "Be ye perfect, even as your

heavenly Father is perfect" (Matt. 5:48). But those who
are seeking perfection are obviously already on their way
towards perfection, else they wouldn't be seeking the kind
of radical progress in holiness that the religious life is meant
to provide. How far along the path to holiness must one
be before thinking of entering religious life? How mature
should a Christian be who wants to profess the evangelical counsels? Is a person who is still struggling with major
sin fit to present themselves for membership in a religious
order, or should a person considering a religious vocation
have attained some minimal level of *ascesis* before considering such a decision?

Let us begin our examination of this question with a
quote from the second Letter of St. Peter:

> ...he hath given us most great and precious
> promises: that by these you may be made partak-
> ers of the divine nature: *flying the corruption of that
> concupiscence which is in the world.* And you, employ-
> ing all care, minister in your faith, virtue; and *in
> virtue, knowledge; and in knowledge, abstinence; and
> in abstinence, patience; and in patience, godliness;
> and in godliness, love of brotherhood; and in love of
> brotherhood, charity.* For if these things be with you
> and abound, they will make you to be neither empty
> nor unfruitful in the knowledge of our Lord Jesus
> Christ. For he that hath not these things with him,
> is blind, and groping, having forgotten that he was
> purged from his old sins. Wherefore, brethren, *labor
> the more, that by good works you may make sure your
> calling and election* (2 Pet. 1:4–10).

Although the passage cited above is directed towards Christians in general, it does have a particular application to those
entering religious life. We see first that when one actively
pursues holiness, one is also fleeing from something else;

"flying the corruption of that concupiscence which is in the world." The religious pursues holiness, but he pursues it by shunning worldliness. This is the classic motive behind the flight to the desert of the Fathers, and it shoots down the sort of sentimentality about religious houses as expressed, for example, in the *Sound of Music* when Reverend Mother tells Maria, "Maria, these walls were not built to shut out problems." I beg to differ, Reverend Mother. Religious houses are not meant to shut out problems *qua* problems, but they were indeed meant to shut out specific sorts of problems, i.e., the "corruption of that concupiscence which is in the world."

So he who would enter religious life ought to be resolved to be done with the corruptions and concupiscence of the world. What does this mean practically? Even if they are still in the world at the time, there should be a firm resolve of avoiding the entanglements of the world and a disdain for that worldly spirit that is evident in an immature soul. In other words, there ought already be present some interior detachment; this interior detachment will be the seed for the exterior detachment that is to follow, and that exterior detachment in turn will strengthen the internal detachment as the soul progresses toward perfection. To what specific degree one needs to be detached is a matter to be addressed with one's spiritual director, but it seems a point of common sense that without some degree of detachment one is not ready to start thinking seriously about the religious life.

But what if that individual is still struggling with serious sin? I am of course not referring to venial sin that every Christian will struggle against so long as they are in the flesh, but sins of a graver nature? There are two interesting points of view here; on the one hand, we could argue that such a person should enter religious life as a means of obtaining the grace necessary to overcoming their weakness; on the other hand, we could say that one should never put themselves under vows to keep strict disciplines when one cannot even keep the commandments in general, even without vows. Both objections have merit; the former focuses on religious life as a means to an end, the latter looks at the religious life as a kind of end in itself.

The truth is that religious life is both. Entering the consecrated life, especially a life of consecrated contemplation, is a sort of end; it facilitates a closeness to God that is about as close as a human in the flesh can get, and to live a life of heroic virtue in the contemplative religious state is a worthy end or aspiration for any Christian. But even this is also a means, insofar as all people are *viators* in this life, a religious vocation lived out well itself is only preparatory and symbolic of the life to come.

Since religious life is both a means and an end of sorts, the answer is that for one who has the constancy of will, as well as a practical plan for combating their predominate fault under the careful eye of a spiritual director, they should not be dissuaded from seeking religious life, "For if the willingness is there, the gift is acceptable according to what one has, not according to what he does not have" (1 Cor. 8:12). We cannot discard the many stories in the lives of the saints of robbers, murderers, and general scoundrels having sudden conversions and immediately joining a monastery. It can happen, although in the stories it usually happens with the personal involvement of a saint as well.

But we must also recall that the novitiate serves as a forge in which the soul gets to test and see if the prayers, rules, disciplines, and guidance of their novice master aid them. The novitiate is meant to weed out those who are not called to the religious life or, conversely, confirm the call in those who are by granting them the special graces they need to overcome their faults and take their place as full members in the religious community. Religious orders do not need people who are holy, but wholly committed with a good will to try and *become* holy, or at least docile to formation. The important things, as the quote from St. Paul above points out, is that the willingness and resolve is there. If that alone can be given to God, any mountain can be moved.

We should understand that the two issues regarding one's desire for holiness and discerning a religious call are very intimately connected and affect each other. Lack of mortification or docility to God's grace makes it less clear if one has a vocation to begin with; an unmortified person has great difficulty in distinguishing the gentle leading of the spirit from his own ideas and emotions. Conversely, a person who practices *ascesis*, even while in the world, is more likely to discern accurately a call from God and make decisions based on the proper motivations after considering the cost with great prudence.

We need not be saints to be religious, but we must want to be. But if we cannot even seriously make this effort in the lay state, we are not fit to present ourselves.

He that is faithful in that which is least, is faithful also in that which is greater: and he that is unjust in that which is little, is unjust also in that which is greater (Luke 16:10).

35

Doubt and the Christian Faith

❧

Since the age of Descartes, doubt has become fashionable. When Descartes introduced methodical doubt as a
means to certainty, the intentional application of doubt has
been the hallmark of the sophisticated. From the philos-
ophes of the Enlightenment who adopted a position of
radical skepticism toward divine revelation, to the modern
scientific establishment that doubts even the rationality of
the human mind, doubt has become the lens through which
modern man views reality. Doubt has become so entrenched
in the mindset of modernity that it has seeped into Christian thought, which has tended to baptize doubt as a virtue.
This often appears under the guise of confusing doubt with
the "dark night" of Catholic mysticism. This is somewhat
understandable: the dark night occurs at a stage of spiritual
development when God removes all sensible reminders
of His presence. Doubt, too, is experienced as a deprivation—a deprivation of certainty.

The two, however, are vastly different. In this essay, we
shall contrast doubt with the traditional dark night and
demonstrate that, while the latter is often a sign of emerging
holiness, the former is nothing Christians ought to celebrate
as a virtue.

Let us begin by considering doubt and its relation to
faith. What is doubt? Doubt is a state in which the mind

is suspended between contradictory propositions and finds itself is unable to assent to either of them. It is opposed to certitude. In the natural order, it is generally related to the degree of evidence in favor of or against a proposition. Doubt arises in one of two ways: that is, it is said to be negative or positive. *Negative* doubt means that there is absence of sufficient evidence for either proposition, making it impossible to render a judgment. *Positive* doubt means the evidence in favor of each proposition is equally strong, making assent to either proposition impossible.

Notice the intrinsic connection between doubt and the presence (or absence) of sufficient evidence. Presumably, if the evidence for any proposition were sufficient, the person would no longer be in doubt about it. The doubt would give way to opinion, and if the evidence were strong enough, to certainty. But when the evidence is deficient in some way, the intellect cannot perceive the truth of a proposition and thus cannot assent. The inability to definitively assent is the state of doubt.

Notice also that doubt is distinct from denial. A person who denies a proposition has certitude, but their certitude is in the proposition's falsity. To deny is to express certitude *against* a proposition. A person in doubt, on the other hand, lacks certitude in either the truth of the or falsity of the proposition. They are suspended between contradictory positions and unable to find any certitude because the evidence is deficient, either in a positive or negative sense.

The question then becomes, what is the relationship of doubt to religion, specifically to Christianity? And is there a positive place for doubt within the Christian framework?

We must first remind ourselves that Christianity is a revealed religion, the assent to which is grounded not in knowledge of empirical propositions, but in faith. Faith is a type of assent that is based neither on empirical evidence nor on the intrinsic rationality of a proposition, but on the authority of the one who speaks. One who assents in faith assents not to evidence but to a person. The First Vatican Council defined the assent of faith as proceeding from the authority of God, who reveals the Christian religion:

> This faith, which is the beginning of human salvation, the Catholic Church professes to be a supernatural virtue, by means of which, with the grace of God inspiring and assisting us, we believe to be true what He has revealed, *not because we perceive its intrinsic truth by the natural light of reason, but because of the authority of God himself, who makes the revelation and can neither deceive nor be deceived* (Sess. III, Chap. 3).

So faith is not dependent or derived from any sort of empirical evidence. This means that when we are discussing faith, doubt has no place. Doubt exists due to an insufficient amount of evidence for a proposition; but articles of faith do not depend upon empirical evidence, but rather on the authority of God. An article of faith must either be accepted or rejected; it cannot be doubted. This is why the *Catholic Encyclopedia* notes, "It follows that doubt in regard to the Christian religion is equivalent to its total rejection, the ground of its acceptance being necessarily in every case the authority on which it is proposed, and not, as with philosophical or scientific doctrines, its intrinsic demonstrability in detail."[1]

This means that doubt never has a positive value in Christianity; it is never an admirable thing to doubt articles of faith. Since articles of faith cannot be "doubted" in the strict sense, doubt amounts to rejection. The *Catholic Encyclopedia* continues:

---

[1]   A. Sharpe, "Doubt," in *The Catholic Encyclopedia* (New York: Robert Appleton Company, 1909). Retrieved June 22, 2016 from New Advent: http://www.newadvent.org/cathen/05141a.htm

> The unconditional, interior assent which the Church demands to the Divine authority of revelation is incompatible with any doubt as to its validity...Doubt as to the Faith is thus impossible in the Catholic Church without infringing the principle of authority on which the Church itself depends...It will be evident from what has been said that doubt cannot coexist either with faith or knowledge in regard to any given subject; faith and doubt are mutually exclusive, and knowledge which is limited by a doubt, becomes, in regard to the subject or part of a subject to which the doubt applies, no longer to knowledge but opinion.[2]

It is understood that persons may suffer from doubt against their will, or they may intentionally cultivate a skeptical disposition of doubt. But in either case, doubt is ultimately something that is antithetical to faith and should not be praised.

Why do we insist on this notion that doubt is antithetical to faith and ought not be praised? Because, as we mentioned above, doubt has become so prevalent throughout modernity that many Christians suffer from it. And—to some degree—Christianity has tried to cope with the age of doubt by baptizing it into a positive virtue.

Occasionally it will come to light that some great figure of modern spirituality struggled with serious doubts about his faith, or suffered what is commonly called a "crisis of faith." And people—understandably wanting to be able to affirm these people as heroes—will praise them for their crisis of faith, as if struggling through a prolonged period of doubt is something to be celebrated. Experiencing doubt or having a "crisis of faith" (which could be defined as a period

---

[2] A. Sharpe, "Doubt."

of prolonged doubt about the faith) is often equated with the "dark night" of Catholic spiritual tradition.

The dark night, however, is something very different from a crisis of faith. A crisis of faith occurs when a person is perturbed by nagging doubts about one or more articles of faith. As we have seen above, doubt is an inability to assent based on a deficiency of evidence. Since faith is not subject to judgments based on evidence but on authority, a crisis of faith signifies a person is wavering between accepting or rejecting the claims of Christianity. It is beyond the scope of this article to go into how one comes out of a crisis of faith, or the character of faith as a gift of God, but it suffices to say that wavering between belief and unbelief is not an admirable position for a Christian to be in.

If a crisis of faith is a state where faith suffers due to persistent doubt, a dark night is a period when faith is strengthened by the soul's increased reliance on God. Traditionally, the dark night is a state of spiritual growth in which all tangible or sensory indicators of God's grace are removed, leaving a soul with a feeling of extreme dryness or spiritual aridity. Deprived of all sensible signs of God's favor, the soul is compelled to cling to God purely by faith. It is a means God uses to refine and strengthen faith by removing all external props to it.

Thus, a dark night is fundamentally different than a crisis of doubt. In a dark night, the believer does not lose faith but rather loses external consolations. A dark night strengthens belief whereas in a crisis of faith it wavers. The dark night does not involve doubting articles of faith; rather, the articles are clung to more tenaciously as sensory consolations dry up. A crisis of faith, on the other hand, means the person is plagued by doubt. And finally, while a dark night is a sign of a spiritually sensitive soul in an advanced state of purgation towards holiness, a crisis of faith often indicates a spiritually unsteady soul whose faith may be in trouble. The

185

dark night and the crisis of faith may seem similar in the sense that they are both experienced as deprivations, but that is where their similarity ends.

As we can see, it is nothing to celebrate when a Christian is in a crisis of faith or period of prolonged doubt. Doubt is not something to be celebrated as a mark of holiness, much less put forward as something normative for a Christian's faith.

To give an example. Suppose—just for the sake of argument—we had an ecclesiastical prelate who made the following comment:

> [Christians who] have not experienced a crisis of faith are missing something. On many occasions I find myself in a crisis of faith. Sometimes I've questioned Jesus and even doubted. Is this really the truth? Is it a dream?" [This happened when I was] a boy, a seminarian, a religious, a priest, a bishop and even now as Pope.[3]

If this statement was really made—if a prelate ever suggested that it was normal or admirable for a Christian to have doubt in Jesus, or to say that Christians who never doubted Jesus were "missing something"—that prelate would be fundamentally in error about the praiseworthiness of doubt.

And what of the faith of this prelate himself, who would boast in his habitual doubt as if it were normal? Given that doubt and faith oppose each other, we would conclude that the faith of this man was fundamentally shaky. Giving him the benefit of the doubt (pun intended) and assuming he has always managed to resolve his doubts in favor of faith, still, his faith would be very imperfect and would in fact be more of a kind of "probable opinion" instead of strict faith.

---

3   http://www.lastampa.it/2016/06/19/vaticaninsider/eng/news/
i-dont-like-it-when-some-speak-of-the-genocide-of-christians-
nO6HzrVDal8dlnjsPg0jdP/pagina.html

The *Catholic Encyclopedia* notes that faith that is nevertheless punctuated by doubt has more in common with opinion than belief:

> ...doubt is sometimes said to imply belief; though such belief or practical certainty *cannot properly be held to rise above the most probable kind of opinion.*[4]

The *Catholic Encyclopedia* is certainly not authoritative, of course, and we cannot judge this prelate's soul, except to say that it is hardly laudable for a Catholic prelate to boast of his habitual doubt in Jesus Christ—and it would be horrendously reckless for the faithful, enamored by this prelate's reputation for piety, to praise this statement as if it were evidence of holiness. This would not be a sign of holiness or heroic faith, but of a faith so shaken by uncertainty that it had degenerated to the level of mere opinion. Or so it would seem.

---

4   Sharpe, "Doubt."

36

Fides Quaerens Intellectum

❧

I see it everywhere. I see it in the online threads of trads debating the powers of the papacy. I see it in dialogues between Protestants and Catholics about the idea of an interpretive authority for divine revelation. I see it in the brain-dump posts of skeptics and the wavering questioning the very concept of religious faith. I see it in the tedious, dreary, back-and-forth discussions between Catholics and Orthodox. It is ubiquitous in religious discussions today.

I am speaking of a hyper-rationalistic approach to matters of faith that insists upon absolutely incontestable logical demonstrations for every point of belief before it is deemed worthy of assent. I refer not to the mere expectation that faith be logical, nor people's reasonable expectation to be convinced of what they are asked to believe; rather, I am referring to people wanting every point of faith to be proven to them in unassailable rational exactitude before they grant it any credibility. What's more, there is the implicit assumption that a point of faith that cannot be proven with ironclad, indisputable, logical certainty is *ipso facto* untrustworthy. This way of thinking is very damaging to faith, as it imposes burdens upon faith it was never meant to carry. Essentially, faith and reason are getting muddled. The propositions of faith are being treated as propositions of logic that must be logically demonstrable in order to have credibility.

Though I see this as foundational, I think we should nevertheless revisit the nature of faith and the type of certainty faith affords, because it seems to me that people on all sides are subjecting faith to the methodology of reason, with the effect that the entire edifice of belief is being treated as one enormous logical demonstration.

Faith and reason are both modes of knowledge. Reason pertains to what we can know from our own powers of observation, whether empirical or logical. Faith pertains to what we know based on the authority of someone else. Both are true ways of knowing, but each is grounded in a different certainty. The certainty of reason is as good as our own powers of observation and intellection; the certainty of faith is as good as the person in whom we put our faith. Whereas reason implies logical deduction, faith implies confidence. Faith itself is an act of trust.

If we go back to the First Vatican Council's dogmatic constitution on the Catholic Faith, *Dei Filius*, we see the following comment on the nature of faith:

> We believe that the things which He has revealed are true; not because of the intrinsic truth of the things, viewed by the natural light of reason, but because of the authority of God Himself who reveals them, and Who can neither be deceived nor deceive (*DF*, III).

When *Dei Filius* says, "We believe...not because of the intrinsic truth of things viewed by the light of natural reason," it does not mean that the propositions of faith are illogical; rather, it means it is not their inherent logical intelligibility that convinces us to believe. Rather, we believe based on the authority of the one who reveals—in this case, Jesus Christ. But to use a more everyday example, if my mother tells me a story about getting ice cream with her father at the fair when she was a little girl, I believe her not because the truth of her assertion is immediately apparent to my intellect, but because I know my mother and I trust *her*. Because of my confidence in her trustworthiness, I assent to her story; I believe it on faith.

Indeed, sometimes faith is the *only* way to know about a thing. In the story above, suppose I subjected my mother's story to the rigorous standards we apply in logic: "Well ma'am, that's a fine story, but is there anyone that can corroborate it? Your father? Oh, he's dead? Well, can you produce any other eyewitnesses? Hmm...it was in 1961, you say, and no one else you knew was present? Convenient. Are there any photographs? Journal entries? How about this fair... where was it? Ah...you don't remember the exact city it was in. I see. Do you remember the name of the company that put the fair on? Well, if I knew the exact date this happened, maybe I could check some archives and...oh what's that? You don't recall the date from sixty-one years ago? What's that? It might have been 1962 or 63 now that you think about it? Ma'am, you must admit, this story sounds incredibly suspicious. Your entire account is full of gaps; I can't understand how you expect me to believe this."

Propositions of faith were never meant to be logical demonstrations. Of course, in the Catholic religion, our core articles of faith fit into the same category as the above example—the Trinity, the Incarnation, the salvific death of Jesus Christ, the grace of baptism, His real presence in the Eucharist, etc. are all truths we would have no way of knowing had they not been revealed. They *require* faith to accept.

But the Christian faith is not illogical, nor was it meant to be blind. Faith does not depend upon reason; but it is in accord with reason. We do not believe because we understand, but as St. Anselm said, we believe so that we may understand. *Fides quaerens intellectum* ("faith seeking understanding"), to use the formula attributed to St. Augustine.

Faith is logical, but not logic-based. It corresponds to reason, but is not derived from it.

That this might be clearer, God gives certain "exterior proofs" to aid our reason, called *motives of credibility*. These motives of credibility do not establish the truth of the faith in a logical sense, but they do testify to it. *Dei Filius* says:

> Nevertheless, in order that the obedience of our faith might be in harmony with reason, God willed that, to the interior help of the Holy Spirit, there should be joined exterior proofs of His revelation; to wit, divine facts, and especially miracles and prophecies, which, as they manifestly display the omnipotence and infinite knowledge of God, are most certain proofs of His Divine Revelation, adapted to the intelligence of all men (*DF*, III).

While we should certainly not assent to something we are not convinced of, we should likewise understand that the faith does not demand every single jot and tittle be accounted for before assent can be given. Faith is a form of knowledge, but it is imperfect, characterized by a "not yet-ness;" "for now we see in a mirror but dimly" says St. Paul (1 Cor. 13:12). "Wrestling" with various problems is an inherent aspect of faith. Faith will always be riddled with difficulties. But, to quote St. John Henry Newman, "Ten thousand difficulties do not make one doubt." Being tripped up with a "difficulty" that you wrestle with is not an argument against assent, nor does it constitute doubting the faith. The motives of credibility help by lending intellectual weight to our assent, creating a momentum towards belief that encompasses the intellect and will. But, we should never confuse the motives of credibility with the act of faith itself. Newman said, "Ten thousand difficulties do not make one doubt;" but we say, "I will continue to doubt, so long as even one difficulty remains unresolved."

I have deliberately chosen not to mention where I have seen this sort of thing happening because I don't want to drag particular individuals into it, but it is going on all over the place. And I see people's faith being wrecked by it left and right. We are always our own worst enemy.

37

Box Checking[†]

✤

In my two decades as a Catholic, I have come to suspect
that many people are fundamentally insecure about their
faith. Not in the sense that they don't believe or lack piety;
rather, in the sense that they are profoundly uncomfortable with the freedom that the faith imposes upon them.
While it is faddish to complain about the burdens and rules
of Catholicism, it is the *liberty* of Catholicism that truly
unnerves people.

It is superficial to see Catholicism as a cluster of oppres-
sive rules. Yes, we have rules. But they leave a considerable amount left to personal judgment, as well. Do I have
a vocation to the priesthood or consecrated life? What
devotions should I commit myself to? What penances
should I undertake? How often and how intense? What is at
the root of my particular vices? What habits of life will best
help me overcome them? How can I deepen my spirituality?
Who should I take on as a spiritual director? What is the
best way to interact with people in my life who disturb my
peace? How can I sincerely forgive those who have wounded
me? In what ways can I best evangelize those around me?
What does God ask of me in my current state in life?

These are all routine judgments any serious Catholic

[†]   Previously unpublished essay.

must make, not even counting the additional questions the chaos in the Church imposes upon us: how should I react to the crises I see around me? To what degree do I owe obedience in situations where the integrity of the faith is being compromised? If I am going to a Novus Ordo parish, how can I nudge my pastor towards tradition without being a pest? If I go to an exclusively TLM parish, what will I do if my access to the traditional Mass is curtailed? How can I effectively pass on the traditions of the faith to my children in a world so hostile to them?

As you see, Catholicism presents us with a vast array of opportunities to exercise our freedom across every facet of life. Ideally, we use our reason trained under prudence to make the optimal decisions in forging our spiritual path, trusting in the providence of God to direct our steps through the mist.

I think *this* is precisely what frightens people, for to truly take initiative for one's own spiritual journey is a terrible responsibility. The thought of having to bear this responsibility is too much for some people; they would rather simply be told what to do. They would prefer to be given a list of tasks that can be checked off. It is easy to conceive of Catholicism as a list of boxes to be checked. This is especially prevalent in traditional Catholicism, where there exists a sort of trad sub-culture identifiable by certain social indicators—Wife only wears dresses? Check. Homeschooling kids? Check. Smoke a pipe or cigars? Check. Beer and liquor aficionado? Check. G.K. Chesterton quotes? Check. Crusader pics on social media profiles? Check. Homesteading? Check. Listen to traddy podcasts? Check.

There is nothing wrong with these things whatsoever. But if we are not careful, it is easy to conceive of our Catholic faith as consisting in such things. To do so is vastly easier than actually making progress in the spiritual life. Which is easier, to dedicate time to prayer and introspection to rooting out one's vices, or to complain about the Novus Ordo online? Water follows the path of least resistance, and so does the human heart unless it is trained under constant discipline.

The problem is we want a blueprint to follow that will *guarantee* us an outcome. We want certainty that if we homeschool our kids they won't deal with same sex attraction. Certainty that if we homestead and only eat unprocessed food we will have better health. Certainty that if we go to the Traditional Latin Mass our children will keep the faith. Certainty that if we follow whatever recommendations Fr. Trad-Priest has for godly courtship our marriages will be happy. We want certainty that if we just do *this*, we will with surety receive *that*.

Of course, I would never deny that certain courses of action yield objectively better results than others. The problem comes when we try to treat these actions like an algorithm, transmuting the virtue of prudence into something formulaic, an input-output machine that yields guaranteed results while absolving us of having to put in the work.

"My paths are not your paths," says the Lord, "and my ways are not your ways" (Isa. 55:8) The Lord has laid upon us things with which we must wrestle. Maturity in the Christian faith comes precisely from grappling with the big questions about our life, learning the virtue of prudence in the school of Christ, that we might learn, "precept upon precept, line upon line, here and little, there a little," (Isa. 28:10) to see things the way God sees, slowly transforming our natural sight into supernatural sight. These things cannot be reduced to mere formulae.

The problem is that we do not want to develop prudence. We do not want to use the principles of our faith under our own judgment to sort out the best way to, say, find a spouse or raise a child. We want someone to hand us a checklist and say, "Just do this and it will all work out." We don't want to grapple with the burden that freedom imposes on us—with the corresponding responsibility if we should make a misstep.

Of course, we should be docile to the guidance of others, especially the saints whom the Church proposes for our models. But even so, the reason we have these role models is to serve as lights that we might find our *own* way. The saints cheer us in running our race, but at the end of the day, *we* must run the race set before us (cf. Heb. 12:1–2). And the track is not always clear; it is not always a matter of following a clearly defined set of directions. The spiritual life is not an IKEA product that comes with illustrated specifications. Recall that God called Abraham out of Ur to sojourn in the Promised Land, but He provided him with no specific itinerary. In all Abraham did and endured throughout his long life, most was left to his own judgment operating under the direction of human prudence.

When you seek guidance, then, seek not for someone to simply tell you what to do—seek rather that the Spirit of God would enlighten your mind and develop in you, through the vicissitudes of life, a robust prudence enabling you to discern what is the best path to take. Do not be afraid of taking responsibility for your own spiritual journey. Holiness is the maturation of Christian virtue under the tutelage of the Holy Spirit which "blows where it wills" (cf. John 3:8); it should not be turned it into a matter of box-checking.

38

Eyes to See

❧

It is easy in these days of darkness to become overwhelmed with despair. Things are a mess; it is hard to find stability anywhere. The socio-economic order we have known for generations is collapsing along with the global hegemony of the West. Our civilization no longer shares an underlying moral consensus about, well, almost anything. And the Church appears impotent to respond. The barque of Peter is tossed upon the storms of the world, and Christ seems asleep in the stern. What can we do?

When we see the waves of darkness crashing upon us all around, when we see so much moral and spiritual devastation, there is a tendency to want to fight strength with strength—to oppose the wave of darkness with an equal but opposite wave of light. They have their media organizations with talking heads, so we need to have our own media and talking heads. They have their publications, we have our publications. They have an aggressive movement, so we will have an aggressive movement. Whatever they have, whatever they throw at us, we will duplicate and put into the service of Christ. We will fight force with force, fire with fire, bull horn with bull horn.

I do not deny that these things have their place, but the struggle will not be won by such means. You cannot defeat Sauron by using the ring against him. The weapons of our warfare are not carnal, St. Paul tells us (cf. 2 Cor. 10:4). The Kingdom of Heaven is qualitatively different than the kingdom of man. Its resources are virtues, prayer its currency; we meet strength with gentleness, pride with humility, mammon with prayer, anger with grace, bigness with littleness. In other words, we make the declaration of St. John the Baptist our own: "He must increase, I must decrease" (John 3:30).

Upon what was Christendom built? Christendom was not built upon the conquests of great warlords, as among the Mohammedans; it was built because regular people sought holiness. It was built because St. Anthony retreated to the desert and St. Benedict to the mountain; because Augustine wept in a garden and Patrick had a dream; because St. Kevin did penance in Luggala Vale, and Columba sailed to fair Iona; because St. Francis took his clothes off and St. Thomas drew an ashen cross on the door of his room. The kingdom of heaven was in the dazzling colors that bewildered Hildegard, in the light that illumined St. Albert's mind as he squinted over a manuscript; in the crosses St. Isaac carved on the trees of Ossernenon; in the little sacrifices of St. Thérèse; in the tears of St. Peter. God was not in the fire nor in the wind, nor in the earthquake, but in the still small voice (cf. 1 Kings 1:19–13).

Now maybe you will say, "Fine and good, but these things can more easily happen within a Christian culture. Since we have neither a Christian culture nor a Church friendly to tradition, these examples are of limited value."

It cannot be denied that Christian culture makes such things easier, but we cannot argue that we first need Christian culture in order to build Christian culture, or that we need a restored Church in order to restore the Church. I don't recall St. Anthony or St. Benedict or St. Francis ever getting anyone's permission before they went into the wilderness. Ah, if you only realized the value of your little works of piety done in love! If you only knew how transformative they are, what channels of grace they open up! Then you would stop thinking that the Church or the country or society to be fixed *first* before you can live an authentically Christian life—that if only this were better my spiritual life would be in order. There's no guarantee it would; in fact, if you think that way, it most certainly would not be.

Many Catholics view the 13th century as the apogee of Christian civilization. But the Christians who actually lived in the 13th century thought their situation was so dire that the end of the world must be at hand. Indeed the 13th century was a high point of apocalyptic speculation, rife with foreboding predictions about the imminent rise of the Antichrist. There were no golden ages, and you do not need to live in one in order to be a good Christian.

The parable of the talents teaches us that we are responsible for nurturing the talents entrusted to us by our Lord, whether they be many or few. The corollary to this is that we are *not* responsible for nurturing talents we have *not* been given. Your talent is the sphere of influence you have: your home, your family, job, and parish. This is where the seeds of heaven need to be sown. It is not your job to fix the Church or save the Republic—at least not primarily. If we forget this, if we take upon ourselves too much, we lose sight of the opportunities for grace right before our eyes. "Sufficient for the day is its own trouble," says the Lord (Matt. 6:34). Do we believe that? What would our life look like if we truly did?

The day of salvation is not far off when Church and State shall be restored; it is *now*. The kingdom of God is within; heaven begins today if we begin our walk today with sincerity. We must recall that the kingdom of God is not only an eschatological reality that emerges at the end of time; it is here, among us. It is akin to Kansas in *The Wizard of Oz*: we are there at any time once we will to be there. The Prodigal

Son can turn towards home at any point—he need not even make it all the way, the father is ready to welcome him as soon as he sees him afar off on the road (cf. Luke 15:20).

These truths do not lose their potency just because the Church is in crisis or because the government is in chaos. I am convinced that as things get more chaotic we will need to turn ever more to the Beatitudes, which were given by Christ specifically for the downtrodden and those laboring under oppression. We do not need to save the world and Church; we need to become saints. And if we pursue this with sincerity—if our intentions are rightly ordered—the world and Church may just be saved as salutary side effects.

Grace is not weakened. God's arm is no less strong to save now than it has ever been. The darkness is ultimately not relevant to what you need to do here and now. All you need is eyes to see.

39

Awash in Glory†

❦

W hen we are young and learning the fundamentals of
our faith, one of the first concepts we absorb about
God is that He is omnipresent, meaning He is "everywhere."
This facet of God's existence seems so simple and straight-
forward that, for most of us, that is the end of it. We don't
feel the need to peer into it any further. We don't struggle
with God's omnipresence the way we struggle with matters
such as the problem of evil or divine providence. "God is
everywhere" seems very basic.

And yet, if we take the time to delve more deeply into
this truth, we may find it a treasure trove of spiritual insight
that can help us see the glory of God that surrounds us.

People often lament the apparent inactivity or absence
of God from their lives. They read stories of miracles from
the Bible or lives of the saints and think, "If I had witnessed
something so miraculous, my faith would never waver."
When hearing of the extraordinary favors and graces God
has given other souls, they think, perhaps with a twinge
of envy, "I wish God would manifest Himself like that to
me." They long for some life-altering theophany that will
lift them from their struggles and push them over the finish
line to sanctity.

---

† Previously unpublished essay.

"Truly thou art a God who hidest thyself," says the prophet (Isa. 45:15). But that is not the end of the story. "It is the glory of God to conceal things, but the glory of kings is to search things out" (Prov. 25:2)—and in Christ, we are all royal, "kings unto our God" (Rev. 5:10). Though God may seem hidden, He shows Himself to those who seek Him in spirit and truth. Those who seek shall find; that which is hidden will be revealed, and those who knock shall have the door opened unto them.

But we must look in the right place. We are told that the prophet Elijah once witnessed a fierce wind, then an earthquake, and then a fire—but God not in the wind, nor the earthquake, nor the fire. Rather, He was found in the "still, small voice" (1 Kgs. 19:12). God wants us to learn to see Him in the ordinary, to recognize Him in the everyday things of life. This is, after all, what distinguishes the saints from everybody else—they have learned to see God's hand in all things, even the seemingly mundane.

Contemplating God's omnipresence can be of great help here. Many years ago, when I was just beginning my studies of Catholic theology, I was taking a college class on aesthetics, the philosophy of beauty. Our professor had us read a little book called *An Introduction to the Metaphysics of St. Thomas Aquinas*, which was a collection of Aquinas's writings on the subject of being with an introduction by Fr. W. Norris Clarke, S.J. This book was my first exposure to St. Thomas's teaching on the real distinction between essence and existence—essence denoting what a thing is, and existence being a verb, the act of *esse* by which a thing exists.

Any Catholic who studies theology is bound to come across this principle at some point, but for me it was no mere abstraction—understanding the act of *esse* profoundly changed the way I interacted with reality.

We know God is omnipresent, but *how* is He omnipresent? This question is tricky because, while we know God is everywhere, for we are not pantheists; God is everywhere, but He is not in everything in any substantial sense. How, then, are we to understand God's presence to all things?

God is present to all things in the sense that He continually holds all things in existence. Everything from the smallest pebble to the most immense star is being held in existence by an act of God. It is this act of God alone which holds them in being and prevents them from falling back into the nothingness from which all matter first emerged. "If he should take back his spirit to himself, and gather to himself his breath, all flesh would perish together, and man would return to dust" (Job 34:14–15).

Aquinas accordingly says that God is truly present in all things, but in terms of His activity. "A thing is wherever it operates. But God operates in all things," he says. "Therefore, God is in all things" (*ST*, I, q. 8, art. 1). He explains, with great precision and beauty, that the existence of all things is an effect of God's own existence. Aquinas says:

> Now since God is very being by His own essence, created being must be His proper effect; as to ignite is the proper effect of fire. Now God causes this effect in things not only when they first begin to be, but as long as they are preserved in being; as light is caused in the air by the sun as long as the air remains illuminated. Therefore as long as a thing has being, God must be present to it, according to its mode of being (*ST*, I, q. 8, art. 1).

This means that God is present to all things in the most intimate way, at the level of their innermost being, holding them in existence. Aquinas concludes his thoughts on God's presence to all things with this beautiful reflection:

> Being is innermost in each thing and most fundamentally inherent in all things since it is formal in

> respect of everything found in a thing, as was shown above. Hence it must be that God is in all things, and innermostly (*ST*, I, q. 8, art. 1).

If this does not inspire us with wonder, then we need to pause and consider the import of these words. The innermost being of everything we encounter in this world is the locus of a direct act of God—the act by which He causes the thing to exist. Walk outside and look around you; that tree, this stone, those bushes, the moss on the bricks—at the heart of each is a divine act of *esse*, existence itself bubbling up as an effect of God's own uncreated being. Everything from the grandest mountain to the most minute flower is the object of a divine action that makes God present to it and all things.

I recall what a profound difference this realization made on my perception. It was as if a veil had been pulled back, revealing the beauty deep within all things. I walked about in a daze, as it were, mystified by the continuous act of *esse* unfolding at the center of all I perceived. I could never see the world the same; every object, even the most mundane, seemed ennobled. Even dark and barren trees upon the mountainside in winter seemed mysterious significations of God's presence to creation.

How would your view of the world change if you kept cognizance of this reality in your day-to-day life? Would you not perceive the world as utterly awash in the glory of the Lord? Would not the evils, sufferings, and challenges of life seem less imposing before the grandeur of God's glorious sustenance of all creation? Would we not find it easier to see the splendor inherent in all things? Would we not cry with the angels, "Holy, holy, holy is the Lord God of hosts; the whole earth is full of His glory" (Isa. 6:3)? Would not the words of Habakkuk find fulfillment in us, which say, "The earth will be filled with the knowledge of the glory of the Lord, as the waters cover the sea" (Hab. 2:14)?

The philosophers tell us that beauty is coextensive with being. If this is true, then we are empowered to see beauty to the degree that we can contemplate being, and vice versa. If all things, at their core, are held in being by an act of *esse* flowing from the being of God Himself, how can we fail to see the beauty all around us? How can we fail to experience the world as a constant eruption of God's glory?

Truly, as I live, all the earth shall be filled with the glory of the Lord (Num 14:21).

40

Response to Robert

🍀

My dear brother, I am touched by your correspondence. I commend you for your candor and openness. You brought up many points, to which I don't know if I will have adequate answer; but I will answer as I can, according to my poor ability. Please understand that my words here represent my own peculiar spiritual approach to the vicissitudes of life. I am no spiritual advisor and do not intend to lecture you on how you ought to be doing things; I am just one beggar telling another beggar where I have found some bread.

You spoke candidly of your fear that your children may one day apostatize. I understand the anxiety a father experiences over their children's faith; I have suffered with it myself occasionally, although—thanks be to God—it is something I no longer fret over. Certainly not because the world has gotten any better. The world is as bad as it ever was, maybe worse. Rather, it has served me well to remember what Christ has said: "Sufficient for the day is its own trouble" (Matt. 6:34). If I wish to have peace, my focus must be on what is before me. The only moment I have any control over is the present, and this is where our Lord desires us to keep our focus. *Now* is the day of salvation; now is the moment of grace. What good can come of anxiety over a future that has not happened, and may never happen? The best way I can secure my children's faith in the future is to be Christlike *now*.

It is easy to get bogged down by the weight of the world's problems. We can feel torn, as if the survival of western civilization depends on our own meager efforts. It sounds as though this has affected you to a degree. But we imagine our theater of action is vastly broader than it is; in actuality, it is quite small, confined to the tiny, fleeting moment we retain control over, a moment so brief it is gone by the time we even conceive of it. But it is to our great benefit that the window is so small, for it puts our salvation into a context we can manage. The grand arc of my life, my eternal destiny, and that of my children and friends, and the will of God overarching it all—it's all too much for me to maintain in head and heart; "such knowledge is too wonderful for me; far too lofty for me to reach" (Ps. 139:6). Thank God He does not ask me to navigate such a tremendous vessel all at once! Rather, he commits to me a single oar and tells me, "Row well, and live;" he entrusts me with a single coin and says, "Use this wisely." And *that* I can manage, especially with the aid of His grace which enlightens my mind. The burden of our salvation is actually quite small: "My yoke is easy, and my burden is light" (Matt. 11:30). That's not to say salvation is not of tremendous import, obviously, but it is one of the paradoxes of the Kingdom of God that the import of such a grave matter can be a burden of light and an easy yoke. Just because something is important does not mean it must be draining; I am reminded of Chesterton's famous quip, "Angels can fly because they take themselves lightly." To achieve great things, we must become small. That includes shrinking the locus of our attention in the way Christ suggests in the Beatitudes.

This relates to our Lord's command to be as children. We usually interpret the childlike faith to relate to trust, and this is certainly true, but I think it also relates to our focus.

Children are concerned only with what is before them; they take no care for tomorrow and scarcely remember yesterday. Their attention is entirely fixated upon whatever they are doing at the moment. Imagine if your own spiritual attention was so fixated on the moment! Invest that kind of focus in the here and now and you will do better. "Which of you by being anxious can add one cubit unto the measure of his life?" (Matt. 6:27).

I realize this is easier said than done, especially given the darkness that is overtaking the world. You mention your disgust with the world increasing with each passing year. But as if this isn't bad enough, you express your fear that your aversion to the world is corrupting your faith with a kind of judgmental self-righteousness. I read this part of your letter many times, contemplating it from various angles, and I think you are correct to be concerned about this matter. Our Lord does not want us to be consumed with disgust, even if we are surrounded by things that truly merit it. Jesus promised that His commandments would bring us *joy*. He said, "If you keep my commandments, you will abide in my love…These things I have spoken to you, that my joy may be in you, and that *your joy may be full*" (John 15:10–11). Our Lord intends our joy to be "full." If we are not people of joy, we therefore must stop and ask why?

The world is covered in darkness, the Church is in chaos, society is adrift, the economy is collapsing. How can we be joyful? I return, again, to my previous theme, reduction of scope; in other words, my brother, who told you any of this was your concern? Has God laid it upon you to save the world? Are the goings on of the Vatican your personal responsibility? Or are the economy and western civilization entrusted entirely to your hands? Assuredly not. Of course, there are some men whose responsibilities are much vaster; some men have been given ten talents, and their obligations are weighty. But such is not you, and such is not me. The

Church? Not my concern. The country? Not my concern—at least not in the sense of making it all my personal business and wasting my energy fretting about it all. Commending it all to prayer is the best we can do, fulfilling what Paul asks of Timothy, to make prayers and supplications for all in authority (1 Tim. 2:1-2).

Then what *is* my concern? The Lord requires my faithfulness in the things He has entrusted to me. What talents has He put into your hand? Your work, your children, your wife, your parish. All relatively modest, when you think about it; at least vastly more so than worrying about the world, the church, and society. My brother, just be attentive to the little circle of this universe that is under your immediate gaze. Hug your wife and children. Be diligent in your daily tasks. Plant and grow your garden and rejoice in the dirt under your fingers, the greenness of grass, blueness of sky, and the wind on your face. Walk down your road and marvel at the movements of bone, sinew, and limb before the ravages of age deprive you of them. Thank God for the breath in your nostrils.

The small things, the small things, ah, yes, that is where happiness lies, if it lies anywhere. Not in the fire, or earthquake, or roar of wind but in the still, small voice. Find Him there. I understand your restlessness to "do more" and "be more;" believe me! I feel it every day of my life. But the Kingdom of God exists in paradox. If you want to do more, then be less. If you want Him to increase you, then decrease. In the Kingdom of our Lord, the way up is down. Instead of thinking about doing greater things, do average things with greater love. Imbue your routine with meaning, and you may find that a golden tide washes over all of it, and the mundane becomes bathed in glory like a sunbeam falling through your window on a summer afternoon.

You mentioned your consternation that you still have notable shortcomings despite doing the "right things." I see how this alarms you, but I think it alarms you more than necessary. The faith is not a matter of box-checking; certainly, these things you mentioned that are part of your routine (Rosary, First Fridays, Adoration, etc.) are all of great importance. But we delude ourselves if we think things are going to go our way just because we have checked the boxes. There is a "not knowingness" that is inherent to faith; a kind of "not yet"—a haze that caused St. Paul to say, "We see in a mirror yet darkly" (1 Cor. 13:12); this mist must simply be accepted. Embrace your status as a *viator*; we are not yet what we will become (cf. 1 John 3:2). We are pilgrims, whose feet ache, whose brows are beaded with sweat, whose stomachs hunger; and for all our trials, we do not clearly see our destination—but it is sufficient to know we are on the road there. We wrestle with God like Jacob wrestled the angel. You must simply accept this; accept the not-knowingness. Of course, continue to do the "right things," continue to have faith, but abandon any notion that the "right things" are going to yield some specific, concrete result in the here and now. Paradoxically, if you let go of that expectation, you might find things begin to change for you. Things change for us when we stop forcing them; the Spirit works in those realms beyond our mind and strength.

Of course it is only by grace that *any* of us can hang on. But what has comforted me greatly is a passage from 1 Corinthians, in which Paul says, "If the readiness is there, it is acceptable according to what a man has, not according to what he has not" (1 Cor. 8:12). If we yield ourselves to God in sincerity, He accepts our offering based on what we *have*, not what we lack. If we invest our talents faithfully, His standard of judgement is proportional to what we had to work with, not what we lacked access to. The man who is given one is only expected to yield one; the man with ten is expected to yield ten. I have returned to this passage again and again to help me see my own life in perspective. I hope it may be of benefit to you as well. That we hang on by grace is nothing to be ashamed of; in fact, it is a tremendous consolation, or at least ought to be.

You spoke also of loneliness. My brother, I understand loneliness all too well. I, too, am a father, but I have been divorced for several years and have no woman. I'm not sure if my loneliness is of the same as yours; I am fairly content where I am at and don't feel the urgent desire for companionship you express. Such was not always the case, though; I have spent many years learning the art of happiness. St. Paul says he had learned to be content in all situations (cf. Phil. 4:11–13). I have realized over time that I, too, can be happy despite my circumstance. I can be happy even in my loneliness. Just like I can have faith even when I don't understand. I can have hope even when I feel broken. I can have love even when darkness is crashing around me. I can express jubilation at the wonders of the mundane. We all can.

But your expression of the loneliness your feel at Eucharistic Adoration grieved me. I do not know what to tell you, other than such has not been my experience. But then again, when I come before our Lord, all I expect Him to do is *just be*. I suppose I do not contrast His "affirming" or "speaking" with His "being." When I come before Him, I come unto the ineffable light, that which simply *is*. And in merely beholding Him, He both affirms and speaks all that must be affirmed and all that needs be said. His gaze is transformative. Heaven is the vision of God. The only thing that ever needs to change in light of that vision is me. I pray for your clarity in this matter.

I will say one more thing: when I was a new Christian, I glossed over the Beatitudes because they seemed so simple. Of course I affirmed them and believed them, but they seemed very "basic." I was in a hurry to get onto bigger things. I did not want milk; I was eager for meat. But now I see that what St. Paul said applied to me: "I fed you with milk, not solid food; for you were not ready for it; and even yet you are not ready" (1 Cor. 3:2). I have since gone back to the Beatitudes and found a treasure trove of riches therein, especially of value for maintaining the right balance and proper spiritual focus. I have derived more spiritual benefit from them than I ever thought possible. So I encourage you to interiorize the Beatitudes until they are your very breath and the pulse in your wrist.

I apologize in advance that my answer is so poor. I fear I may not be of much help to you. But know that I have prayed for you in hopes that you, too, may find light, refreshment, and peace in His glory.

Appendix

The essays in this book were first published at Unam Sanctam Catholicam on the following dates:

- *Balancing Truth and Humility*
  (December 26, 2020)
- *Mass Marketing Mysticism* (April 27, 2010)
- *Resisting Temptation* (March 27, 2014)
- *Christ Will Give You Victory* (January 25, 2019)
- *The Greatest Schism* (December 15, 2013)
- *Mortification and Penance* (December 26, 2013)
- *God Loves You* (April 25, 2015)
- *Good, Acceptable, and Perfect Will of God*
  (December 6, 2014)
- *Study on to Salvation* (February 11, 2014)
- *Hearts of Stone to Hearts of Flesh* (March 1, 2015)
- *Eat Dung, Get Sick* (July 11, 2022)
- *Personal Relationship with Jesus* (July 18, 2010)
- *Discouragement from Habitual Sin*
  (November 28, 2021)
- *The Hidden Work of Grace* (November 10, 2021)
- *The Spirit of Lent* (February 28, 2013)
- *The Art of Fasting* (February 10, 2013)
- *The Rosary and Poverty* (October 6, 2014)
- *Joshua the Contemplative* (December 28, 2014)
- *Alcuin to Higbald: A Christian View on Temporal Misfortune* (June 15, 2012)

Appendix

- *Waves of Darkness* (September 12, 2021)
- *The Law of the Harvest* (July 24, 2022)
- *Leniency and Severity* (February 7, 2021)
- *Escaping Our Subjectivity* (August 13, 2021)
- *The Perfecting of Every Work and the Holy Car Ride* (February 17, 2015)
- *The Distraction of That One Sin* (September 22, 2013)
- *The Untruth We All Profess* (May 27, 2014)
- *With the Joy of Christ's First Breath* (April 4, 2021)
- *A Miserable Cup of Coffee* (February 13, 2015)
- *The Dark Mirror of Faith* (March 6, 2022)
- *The Relation of Gluttony and Lust* (October 16, 2011)
- *"I Know That My Redeemer Lives"* (April 7, 2022)
- *True and False Dark Nights* (June 8, 2022)
- *Despair and Presumption* (May 16, 2015)
- *Viators Seeking Perfection* (January 16, 2013)
- *Doubt and the Christian Faith* (June 21, 2016)
- *Fides Quaerens Intellectum* (December 22, 2022)
- *Box Checking* (February 12, 2023)
- *Eyes to See* (December 11, 2022)
- *Awash in Glory* (March 2, 2023)
- *Response to Robert* (September 9, 2022)

About the Authors

Phillip Campbell is a Catholic educator and prolific author, best known for his *Story of Civilization* series from TAN Books, as well as numerous other works on Catholic history and spirituality. He received a BA in history from Ave Maria University and a Certificate in Secondary Education from Madonna University. In 2007, Phillip founded the traditional Catholic blog "Unam Sanctam Catholicam," followed by a website of the same name in 2012. "Unam Sanctam Catholicam" has been a pillar of balanced commentary in the traditional Catholic world since its inception. To date, Phillip has published over 1,500 essays under the "Unam Sanctam Catholicam" label.

dom Noah Moerbeek, CPMO, is the Preceptor and Novice Master for the North American Preceptory of the Militia Templi, commonly known as the Order of the Poor Knights of Christ. dom Noah was a regular contributor to "Unam Sanctam Catholicam" between 2014 and 2017.

Index

www.ingramcontent.com/pod-product-compliance
Lightning Source LLC
Chambersburg PA
CBHW021618120626
46545CB00001B/293